"Carefully written, impeccably researched, biblically attuned, sensitive and thought-provoking, this is a masterful treatment of a vitally important topic. The book is certain to have great relevance for counselors, church leaders, students, researchers and all who have an interest in the complex issues surrounding homosexuality."
GARY R. COLLINS, *CLINICAL PSYCHOLOGIST, AUTHOR*

"This is a brilliant book of common sense, reasoned analysis and biblical wisdom. A must read for every Christian who wants more light than heat on what may be the watershed issue of Christ and culture in this generation."
TIMOTHY GEORGE, *DEAN,*
BEESON DIVINITY SCHOOL OF SAMFORD UNIVERSITY

"Both liberal and conservative Christians are ignorant about scientific studies of homosexuality. Furthermore, most do not understand the contributions and limits of scientific claims to theological-ethical reasoning about Christian morality. This new book by Jones and Yarhouse provides significant insights into both issues and will benefit greatly all sides to the contemporary debate."
DON BROWNING, *DIVINITY SCHOOL,*
UNIVERSITY OF CHICAGO

"How grateful I am to Stanton Jones and Mark Yarhouse for this book. As one engaged now for over twenty-five years in the church's moral debate about homosexuality, it is refreshing to read the results of scientific research that elevates the level of discussion and dispels many rhetorical myths. This is an important read!"
JOHN HUFFMAN, *ST. ANDREW'S PRESBYTERIAN CHURCH,*
NEWPORT BEACH, CALIFORNIA

"A carefully researched and well-balanced critique. In the final chapter the authors show how their moral teaching flows out of their Faith vision, their love of Christ. I recommend this book for all those helping men and women with same-sex attractions to live chastely in the unmarried or married states."
FR. JOHN F. HARVEY, *OSFS, DIRECTOR,*
COURAGE, NEW YORK, NEW YORK

Homosexuality

The Use of Scientific Research in the Church's Moral Debate

Stanton L. Jones
& Mark A. Yarhouse

InterVarsity Press
Downers Grove, Illinois

InterVarsity Press
P.O. Box 1400, Downers Grove, IL 60515-1426
World Wide Web: www.ivpress.com
E-mail: mail@ivpress.com

InterVarsity Press® is the book-publishing division of InterVarsity Christian Fellowship/USA®, a student movement active on campus at hundreds of universities, colleges and schools of nursing in the United States of America, and a member movement of the International Fellowship of Evangelical Students. For information about local and regional activities, write Public Relations Dept., InterVarsity Christian Fellowship/USA, 6400 Schroeder Rd., P.O. Box 7895, Madison, WI 53707-7895.

Cover illustration: Roberta Polfus

ISBN 0-8308-1567-8

Printed in the United States of America ∞

Library of Congress Cataloging-in-Publication Data

Jones, Stanton L.
    Homosexuality: the use of scientific research in the church's moral debate/Stanton L.
Jones & Mark A. Yarhouse.
      p. cm.
    Includes bibliographical references.
    ISBN 0-8308-1567-8 (pbk.: alk. paper)
    1. Homosexuality—Religious aspects—Christianity. I. Yarhouse, Mark A., 1968- II.
Title.
BR115.H6 J66 2000
261.8'35766—dc21

                                        00-059689

19	18	17	16	15	14	13	12	11	10	9	8	7	6	5	4	3	2	1
15	14	13	12	11	10	09	08	07	06	05	04	03	02	01	00			

*To unnamed friends
who, through sharing their
sexual struggles,
have bequeathed to me
a deeper and richer understanding
of what it means to be
a disciple of Jesus Christ.*
Stan —

*To my parents,
Roger and Shyla Yarhouse,
who raised me,
by God's mercy and grace,
to see his Word as
a lamp to my feet and
a light for my path.*
Ps 119:105
Mark —

CONTENTS

Acknowledgments

This book presents, in expanded and hopefully more accessible form, a series of arguments that we have made in a number of different professional contexts. We are grateful for the permission of those who published these earlier works to base the present manuscript on that work.

Chapter one is based on a paper by Stanton Jones entitled "Science and Homosexuality," which was presented to the Lutheran Bishops meeting in the Evangelical Lutheran Church of America's Bishop's Academy in Mundelein, Illinois, on January 12, 1999.

The bulk of chapters two through five were originally presented in a very lengthy manuscript that no one wanted to publish, as it was much too long for a journal article or book chapter, and we had not yet thought of publishing a book on this subject. That material was eventually divided into two separate but intertwined presentations. Much of the material about how denominational documents handle scientific "findings" in their moral arguments eventually found its way into our chapter "The Use, Misuse, and Abuse of Science in the Ecclesiastical Homosexuality Debates," in *Homosexuality, Science, and the "Plain Sense" of Scripture,* ed. David L. Balch (Grand Rapids, Mich.: Eerdmans, 2000, pp. 73-120). The more detailed presentation of the scientific research was published as an article by us titled "Science and the Ecclesiastical Homosexuality Debates," *Christian Scholar's Review* 26, no. 4 (1997): 446-77. A number of arguments from another article of ours have also found their way into the present work, that being "A Critique of Materialist Assumptions in Interpretations of Research on Homosexuality," *Christian Scholar's Review* 26, no. 4 (1997): 478-95. Our presentation of "what science says" in chapters two through five has been brought up to date through January 1, 2000, and has also been most dramatically expanded beyond our earlier presentations in the material presented in chapter five on changing sexual orientation, which includes some material adapted from Mark Yarhouse's "Group Therapies for Homosexuals Seeking Change," *Journal of Psychology and Theology* 26, no. 3 (1998): 247-59 and "Expanding Alternatives for Young Adults Who Experience Same-Sex Attraction: A Systems Perspective," *Marriage and Family: A Christian Journal* 3, no. 2:133-51.

Our concluding chapter in this book is based on a paper by Stanton Jones titled "The Ethical Crisis: Sexual Ethics and Contemporary Christian Culture," which was presented to the Wheaton College Faculty Faith and Learning Seminar in April 1999.

We would like to thank Linda Doll, our editor at InterVarsity Press, for her work in helping us prepare the manuscript. We would also like to thank those who read over the manuscript and offered helpful suggestions: Rodger Bufford, Robert Gagnon, Jim Hoover, Lori Burkett and Lori Yarhouse.

1

Research, Reason
& Religion

It is clear that being a follower of Christ, exhibiting authentic commitment, and allowing the belief-content of that commitment to function as control within one's devising
and weighing of theories are preconditions of arriving at a fully comprehensive, coherent, consistent, and true body of theories in the sciences.
—NICHOLAS WOLTERSTORFF, *REASON WITHIN
THE BOUNDS OF RELIGION*

O *n October 7, 1998, Matthew Shepard, an openly gay twenty-two-year-*
old University of Wyoming student, left a campus bar in a
pickup truck with two men, was tied to a fence outside of town
and then beaten savagely with a pistol.[1] He was left out in
freezing weather for eighteen hours before he was found. He was placed
on a respirator, brain dead, for several days, and died on October 12.

This was a tragic and unconscionable act of violence against another
human being. Any Christian who thinks that such treatment is justified
by Matthew's homosexuality does not understand Christian morality or
God's grace and fails to manifest the Christian virtues and character
that God desires of us. The Matthew Shepard murder has understand-
ably sparked cries of outrage from the homosexual community. Christians ought to be as outraged by such events as any gay rights
advocate.

---

[1]Portions of chapter one were first presented in a paper by Stanton L. Jones titled "Science
and Homosexuality" (presented at the Evangelical Lutheran Church of America's
Bishop's Academy meeting in Mundelein, Illinois, January 12, 1999).

But who is at fault for this sinful treatment of Matthew Shepard? Many would like to use this tragedy opportunistically to convince us that it is the historic Christian judgment that homosexual behavior is immoral that is ultimately at fault in a case like this; that it is the judgment of the apostle Paul recorded in 1 Corinthians that is at fault. You remember his words, of course:

> Do you not know that the wicked will not inherit the kingdom of God? Do not be deceived: Neither the sexually immoral nor idolaters nor adulterers nor male prostitutes nor homosexual offenders nor thieves nor the greedy nor drunkards nor slanderers nor swindlers will inherit the kingdom of God. And that is what some of you *were*. (1 Cor 6:9-10, emphasis added)

Critics want to argue that such a moral judgment is bigotry and *must* be wrong because it is the source of attacks upon and rejection of gay and lesbian persons. Some pro-gay supporters have taken the occasion of Matthew Shepard's death to tie the cause of hate crimes to two factors: (1) the conservative religious view that homosexual behavior is immoral and (2) the offering of "healing" ministry to homosexual persons who are pursuing change of behavior or orientation. For example, in a recent *Christianity Today* news report Elizabeth Birch, director of the gay-rights organization Human Rights Campaign, expresses concern that "endorsing reparative therapy for homosexuals and telling people they have a choice about their sexual orientation is 'hateful.' "[2] The message here suggests that testimonials of change—that some gays have become ex-gays—are merely playing on anti-gay sentiments by communicating a harmful message to the public that gay people are sick and in need of a cure. Others see a more explicit tie between ex-gay advertisements and violent hate crimes: that somehow these anecdotal reports of change communicate the distorted message that homosexuality can be beaten out of people.

Of course, both points are debatable: it is questionable, to say the least, that the historic Christian sexual ethic was even remotely the cause of the attack on Matthew Shepard. Further, it is not at all clear that even if it was, that would constitute grounds for judging this moral stance to

---

[2]Jody Veenker, "Called to Hate? How Antihomosexual Crusader Fred Phelps Discredits the Church," *Christianity Today*, October 25, 1999, p. 89.

be wrong.[3] So despite our current difficulties, we must still engage the central issue: Is homosexual behavior wrong?

We believe in being clear about our assumptions and presuppositions, so we confess that we are defending the historic understanding of the church, grounded in the Bible's teaching, that homosexual behavior is immoral. Let us give away our punch line at the very start: We will show, persuasively we hope, that while science provides us with many interesting and useful perspectives on sexual orientation and behavior, the best science of this day fails to persuade the thoughtful Christian to change his or her moral stance. Science has nothing to offer that would even remotely constitute persuasive evidence that would compel us to deviate from the historic Christian judgment that full homosexual intimacy, homosexual behavior, is immoral.[4]

Views of the Relationship Between Science and Religion

This book is titled *Homosexuality: The Use of Scientific Research in the Church's Moral Debate*. As this title suggests, we are asking the question of how research on homosexuality should inform our understanding of homosexuality, particularly in the church. How should we think about the relevance of scientific evidence to our moral and theological views of homosexual behavior? How can science have any relevance for a religious position?

---

[3]Imagine that an Islamic terrorist attack is launched on innocent American civilians, and the claim is made by the terrorists that their attack was justified by American aid to the nation of Israel. Americans might rightly judge the terrorist attack on the American civilians to be wrong but would not be able to conclude anything about the morality of our support for Israel from the moral status of the terrorist attack. There is no necessary link between the two moral valuations. So even if the Christian moral judgment that homosexual behavior is wrong in some way contributed to the reprehensible treatment of Shepard, that does not mean the Christian moral stance is itself wrong.

[4]Nicholas Wolterstorff writes to Christian scholars on the relationship between faith and theory: "Two fundamental issues face all scholars. They must decide which matters to investigate. And on the matters under investigation, they must decide which views to hold" (*Reason Within the Bounds of Reason*, 2nd ed. [Grand Rapids, Mich.: Eerdmans, 1984], p. 9). Later he articulates the importance of "control beliefs" for Christian scholars: "The religious beliefs of the Christian scholar ought to function as *control* beliefs within his devising and weighing of theories" (p. 70). Consistent with Wolterstorff's exhortation we have aspired to have this book be a case study in good scholarship conducted "through the eyes of faith."

There are three positions on the relationship of science and religion (ones that we reject) that make dialogue between the two suspect or impossible: perspectivalism, imperialism and postmodern relativism.

Perspectivalism is the view that science and religion are two *complementary* ways of knowing (epistemologies) that deal with alternative and distinct vantage points or perspectives on reality. The classic illustration of perspectivalism is the distinction between the technical understanding of an end zone scoreboard of the electrical engineer who designed it and the subjective understanding of the die-hard football fan looking at it to see if there is hope for his or her team to make a comeback. The electrical functioning and structural integrity of the device have nothing to do with the meaning of the messages that flash across it; dialogue about which of the two is the true understanding of the sign would be silly. If we are perspectivalists, our dialogue is really nothing other than talking past each other because there is no real interaction between the perspectives. The person who is both a football fan and electrical engineer may have a more fulsome experience of the score board, but the two perspectives do not really affect each other. Neither can science and religion affect each other, if you are a perspectivalist.

Imperialism is the view that science and religion are *competing* descriptions of the same reality, with one trying to utterly dominate and replace the other. In most formulations, imperialists believe that scientific fact is replacing magical religiosity with each progressive advance of science. Dialogue in such a model is really merely a means for asserting power and displacing the opposing system—scientists dialogue with the religious folks to educate them. This is what is usually at work when science is brought to bear in the "dialogue" about homosexuality. The presumption is that science has the "right stuff" to ground contemporary sexual ethics, whereas religion, which is viewed as outdated superstition, does not. To be fair, there can be imperialism from the religious side too, as when "Bible only" Christians push for the elimination of scientific research that impinges on any religious question, or deny the validity of any scientific research that conflicts with their understanding of how reality should be (such as the finding that not all gay people are desperately unhappy and tormented).

There is a third extreme position that subverts any real dialogue between religion and science. Faith in science as the royal route to truth has been replaced for many today by a postmodern relativism that despairs that truth even exists. Scientific imperialism, mentioned in the previous paragraph, is linked to what has been called modernism (faith in the necessary triumph of human rationality through science). As modernism has faltered, one set of alternatives to the triumph of scientific rationality has come to be called postmodernism. In this view, science's authority has been replaced by the authority of narrative; universal "laws" or "rules" are out and our personal stories, stories that can be true for one person and not for another, are in. In church debates about the morality of homosexual behavior, this stance is often seen in the preference for presentations of dialogue with and stories from gays and lesbians—where stories about a person's experience are given more weight than either science or Scripture. Science has been deconstructed as just another imperialistic narrative structure, one that must be reduced to just another voice in the Babel of voices.

We believe that these three views—perspectivalism, imperialism, and postmodern relativism—are deeply flawed. We are *critical realists*, which means that we believe that there is a real world out there where it is possible to know and know truly (hence, "realism"), but we also believe that our theories and hypotheses about that world, and our religious presuppositions and beliefs about reality, color and shape our capacity to know the world (hence, "critical realism"). This view establishes the possibility of true dialogue between science and religion, a risky dialogue that actually could and does involve science influencing what we believe about religion (as when Galileo changed our view of the physical universe and hence how we understand certain passages of Scripture) *and* religion influencing what we believe about empirical reality (as when our Christian beliefs lead us to view certain aspects of what it means to be human differently than the non-Christian).[5]

We believe that both religious faith and science deal with reality. Although they deal with differing slices of reality, these slices are overlapping. If this claim is true, it would suggest that both religious belief

---

[5]See Stanton L. Jones, "A Constructive Relationship for Religion with the Science and Profession of Psychology: Perhaps the Boldest Model Yet," *American Psychologist* 49, no. 3 (1994): 184-99, and Stanton L. Jones and Richard E. Butman, *Modern Psychotherapies: A Comprehensive Christian Appraisal* (Downers Grove, Ill.: InterVarsity Press, 1991).

and science are likely to be important and informative in our understanding of human life. Science deals with aspects of reality that we can measure, repeat and manipulate (these are what we refer to as *empirical* aspects of reality). Science measures certain events, phenomena and experiences, and reports on what it finds within the limitations of scientific methods of inquiry. But what about religious faith? Like the apostle Paul we believe that Christianity is about two primary sorts of "things": God's acts in the world and God's Word. His acts are events that are historical realities and hence empirical realities of a sort, even if those historical realities cannot be controlled and repeated by the scientist. God's Word is the historical self-revelation in human language from the eternal God of the universe. This linguistic self-revelation makes claims about what is true—claims to which we must respond. If these historic events are fabrications, and if these knowledge claims in God's Word are false, then we are above all people to be pitied because we are deluded.

Science and religion intersect as the realities they examine and about which they make truth claims intersect. There are many areas where there is no such overlap. Many of the topics examined by science are ones about which the Scriptures make no claims; there are no hidden Bible verses about the molecular structure of polymers that we have found. Many of the truth claims of the Scriptures, such as the claim that Jesus changed water to wine or brought Lazarus back from the dead, can neither be confirmed nor refuted by empirical science since these were one-time, unrepeatable events. Such actions were, nevertheless, real actions in a real world, and so a scientist who happened to have been analyzing the water that Jesus turned into wine would have been able to empirically document a fundamental change in chemical composition. Science *does* make truth claims about homosexual behavior and orientation, and Christianity also makes truth claims about homosexual behavior (and about sexuality and human nature more generally), and so it is right for Christians to be informed by both sources of knowledge.

It is thus *right* for Christians to think seriously about what science says about homosexuality, particularly as the church struggles with important and complex questions about the morality of same-sex behavior.

Arguments for the Authority of Science to Overturn Traditional Christian Moral Teaching

Most of those who agree that a dialogue between science and Christian faith is valid and vital are not defenders of the traditional sexual morality of the church. The findings and supposed findings or "facts" of science have been most often used to suggest that the church must abandon its historic moral stance on homosexuality. What rationale can be offered for scientific findings being the ground for revising Christian teaching? Two versions of an argument are typically offered to justify the revision of Christian teaching based on science: that the Bible is wrong and that it is vague.

The Bible is wrong. The first is the argument that the Bible, though it is clear in its teachings about homosexuality, is in *error* on homosexuality. Here is how the argument goes: *The moral teachings of the Bible and the Christian tradition regarding homosexual behavior cannot be considered to be without error and thus must be tested against the fruits of human reason. If modern science proves that the views expressed in the Bible are mere prejudice and ill-founded, we must adapt our views. Through advances in human reason, particularly through modern scientific discovery, we have come to see homosexual orientation as a natural and normal and good human variant. In short, the Bible is wrong on this matter and must be superseded by human reason.*

The Bible is vague. The second argument is that the Bible, though foundational to our Christian ethic, is *inconsistent* and *vague* on homosexuality. The Bible cannot really be accused of being wrong because what it says is so confused that it really does not amount to a consistent teaching. The argument here is that, in direct parallel to what some see as the internal tension in the Bible's teachings about women in ministry, *the Bible and Christian tradition reveal substantial confusion and inconsistency on the moral evaluation of homosexual behavior. In the face of this lack of clarity, we must look to our contemporary understanding to make rational decisions about sexual morality.*

One specific variation of this second argument deserves closer scrutiny. Some argue that if the Bible is inconsistent and vague, then it can provide only general moral guidance for us as we think about sexual ethics. In other words, we should ignore *specific* biblical commands about specific sexual behaviors and turn instead to *general* themes of love and justice—general virtues that are clear, relevant and binding today. One problem is that this was certainly not the view of our Lord himself of the

Scriptures, and it is out of line with the church's historical understanding of God's revelation of himself and his will to us. Proponents of this view, in order to make it work, need to specify an authority that can guide them in determining whether they are acting in a way that is loving and just (since they no longer have the specific rules of Scripture to serve that function). Most conclude that this authority is that of their own experience or intuition, their own sense of inner "rightness." The logic might be summarized simply as follows:

1. God has made me and therefore made the desires I have.
2. Everything God makes is good, and therefore my desires are good.
3. Good desires deserve to be, even *ought* to be, fulfilled.[6]

The problem with this logic is that every point is false. The Christian church has never taught that all our desires come from God, has never taught that all our desires are good and has never taught that every desire, even every good desire, ought to be fulfilled. A heterosexual man's lust for a woman who is not his wife does not come from God (#1) and is not a good desire (#2), and should not be indulged (#3; the church historically has taught that even the good desire of an engaged man for his fiancée should not be fulfilled before he is married).

These are the common assumptions behind arguments that the church must change its traditional ethical teaching regarding homosexual behavior in light of the findings of science. We reject both of these arguments. Scripture is not in error and is not vague. We approach the dialogue with science as Christians who expect to learn from the findings of science when those findings are carefully examined. Given this contemporary setting for this discussion, we want to touch on three things: (1) the value of dialogue in ethical decision making, (2) the clarity of what the Scriptures say about homosexuality and (3) the nature of the Christian sexual ethic as taught historically by the church.

The Role of Dialogue

The revisionists constantly push for Christian traditionalists to "dialogue" with gays and lesbians. What is the value of dialogue in shaping a Christian sexual ethic? Our Lord was in constant and loving dialogue with every sort of person; we should follow his model. Unlike him, we

---

[6]Our thanks to Alan Jacobs for helping us clarify this logic.

are fallen and can be sadly deluded in our pronouncements of truth; dialogue is necessary as we seek truth and acknowledge that our knowledge of God's truth is ever partial and distorted. Dialogue can be a way of teaching and of learning how to articulate the teaching of the church in a manner relevant to the contemporary context. Dialogue can also be a place where others correct us in our errors. For all these reasons, we should be in dialogue.

But the value of dialogue is qualified by the reality that if we are fallen and can be sadly deluded in our pronouncements of truth, then so also can our partners in dialogue. As we enter a dialogue, we must contend with the possibility that we might come out of the dialogue changed and *more* in error than we were at the start.

Further, much of the push for dialogue comes from those who presuppose that the truth is not fixed, that no one group has a corner on the truth, and that a firm judgment that certain acts are immoral is an arrogant and rejecting and hateful act. The postmodern relativists mentioned earlier believe that one story, one narrative, is no better than another; none can have authority over another. Dialogue becomes a way to get traditionalists to back away from believing that they have a corner on the market on God's truth. Radically incompatible fundamental views of the faith—of revelation, of salvation and sanctification, of church authority, of human nature, of ethics—are often in play in these dialogues, so that there is in fact often no hope for reaching common ground unless fundamental shifts in these theological foundations take place.[7] It is just one person's story against another's. How can a person who believes that God spoke in the words of Scripture and a person who does not believe that the Scriptures are God's authoritative word ever achieve a common understanding?

The ultimate, unavoidable issue is that some source of knowledge and understanding must be privileged, must be given the exalted status of the bedrock that we assume in faith to be trustworthy and reliable. To which source is the Christian church going to grant such privilege? The findings of science at this point in history? Human experience? Human reason? The Scriptures?

---

[7] John Milbank, "The End of Dialogue," in *Christian Uniqueness Reconsidered: The Myth of a Pluralistic Theology of Religions*, ed. Gavin D'Costa (Maryknoll, N.Y.: Orbis, 1990), pp. 174-91.

Clarity of Scripture

Is the Bible clear in what it teaches about homosexuality? Some would claim that it is not clear. True, homosexual behavior is not a major focus of the Scriptures. The list of verses that directly address the subject is only six to eight long, depending on how you define direct. But the passages that do address homosexual behavior speak with one voice on the subject and are *crystal clear in condemning homosexual behavior, male and female, every time it is mentioned.* Further, the church has handled the morality of homosexual behavior with almost amazing consistency, having consistently judged it throughout history as immoral. Yes, you can find the occasional fringe figure who took a deviant perspective on this matter, but such instances are clearly not the norm. And the prohibition on homosexual behavior found in the Bible fits with the broader Christian sexual ethic that we will introduce in a moment and develop in chapter six.

Let us give one concrete example of the clarity of what the Scriptures say on this subject. Critics of the traditional ethical stance that prohibits homosexual behavior used to argue that there was not clear evidence of continuity between what the Old and New Testaments say on this subject. Further, a great deal of importance was placed on the fact that Paul, speaking in 1 Corinthians 6:9 and 1 Timothy 1:10, used a word that had never appeared in Greek before those uses. This word, *arsenokoitai,* translated as "pervert," "homosexual" and "homosexual offender," became the focus of heated debate. This use of the new word *arsenokoitai* gave ground for speculations that Paul did not know of what we understand today as homosexuality, that whatever he was referring to in these passages was not what we are dealing with today, and most importantly, that we had no evidence for New Testament continuity with Old Testament (Levitical) law on this matter.

Recent research[8] has established, however, that the word *arsenokoitai* was created as a direct reference to Leviticus 18:22 and 20:13. In the Septuagint (the ancient Greek translation of the Old Testament with which Paul would have been familiar) the Greek words for "men" (*arse-*

---

[8]See David F. Wright, "Homosexuality: The Relevance of the Bible," in *Readings in Christian Ethics: Issues and Applications,* ed. David K. Clark and Robert V. Rakestraw (Grand Rapids, Mich.: Baker, 1996), pp. 194-202.

nos) and "lay" *(koiten)* occur side by side in these two passages. Paul took a description of action, "men who lay," and turned it into a noun: "man-layers." This not only solves the mystery of the meaning of the word but is sound evidence of continuity between the Old and New Testaments.

The Christian Church's Traditional View of Sexuality: A Sketch

What is the Christian church's traditional view of sexuality? Given the outcry among conservatives around various sexual sins, we might think that this is an easy question to answer. However, this question is actually difficult to answer, at least in part because the views of Christians have, over the millennia, ranged from the sensuality and lasciviousness of the church at Corinth (1 Cor 5:9-13; 6:9-20) to the asceticism of the desert mystics and many of the second- and third-century patriarchs (asceticism looks down on all bodily pleasure, especially the sexual). Further, the Scriptures fail to present the kind of systematized treatment of sexual ethics and the reasoning behind those ethics that so many long for today. Nevertheless, the church, through much of its history, has regarded something like the following brief sketch as its core teaching on sexuality.

The traditional perspective has been that God created us as embodied, physical beings, male and female, and that God created our capacity for sexual union in intercourse. God created each of these aspects of our humanity intentionally, and he called them "very good" on the sixth day of creation. Two of the most important purposes of sexual intercourse are mentioned early in the creation stories—procreation and union where two become one flesh. Other purposes of sexual intercourse include pleasure and the satisfaction of what is regarded as a normal human desire (Prov 5; 1 Cor 7:1-5). It is the purpose or function of union that appears to be most central, as our Lord made this notion of union central to his teaching on divorce and the nature of marriage (Mt 19). Further, Paul speaks of this purpose of union in describing the role that Christian marriage should play in instructing the world about the nature of the relationship between Christ and his church (Eph 5).

Our sexuality, along with all other aspects of life, was marred by the Fall. What had previously been an unadulterated good was now, and forevermore, experienced as a battleground of twisted desires and motives, and an occasion for much suffering. Our sexuality became an arena in which many of the problems of human life are played out, and it became a focus of God's redeeming work. God's redemptive work began through the revelation of the outlines of his moral will for our lives in the Law of the Old Testament. In the moral law God began to rein in the most offensive of human perversions of his beautiful gift of sexuality. Adultery, homosexual behavior, rape, incest, bestiality were all condemned in harsh terms.

How did our Lord Jesus, in his earthly ministry, deal with sexual ethics? The topic was not a major preoccupation of his during his ministry in Palestine. Yet it is notable that, unlike his observance (or lack thereof) and teaching on the ceremonial law, our Lord *never modified any portion of the moral law dealing with sexuality other than to raise the expectations on us.* Our Lord raised the expectations on us by expanding the domain of application of the law of God from what we do externally, with our bodies, to that *plus* what we do with our minds and hearts. Jesus did this by condemning lust with the same vigor as any overt behavior (Mt 5). Jesus himself lived a life of chaste singleness and commended that life as virtuous and a path pleasing to God, yet in his teachings on marriage continued the Jewish pattern of affirming marriage and the unifying gift of sexual intimacy as wonderful gifts from God. Paul and the other apostles continued this pattern of maintaining continuity with Old Testament moral law; we have no historical or textual indication of any fundamental revision of the Hebraic understanding of sexual morality in the life of the early church.

Christians have thus had good reason to regard the following as a reasonable summary of Christian teaching on sexual morality: *God commends chastity within marriage (the enjoyment of one's spouse and the shunning of all other sexual intimacies) and chastity outside of marriage (refraining from impure sexual relations).* These twin teachings have been the foundational sexual norms of our faith community. It is worth noting that the assumptions about the purposes of our sexuality mentioned earlier informed the Christian understanding both of what is moral and immoral and of what is natural and unnatural. With regard to the latter, "natural" was loosely understood as that which was in accord with God's purpose for our sexuality. Homosexual behavior then was wrong: both because it was contrary to the revealed will of God as expressed in the moral law, and because it was unnatural, in that it could not well serve all of the purposes for which our sexuality was given.

We want to suggest that given the clarity of Scripture, and given the historical consistency of the church's sexual ethic, the burden of proof is on those who want to change the church's historic position to make a strong case for change. Those who want to change the church's position have failed to date to produce a compelling case.

Recent Developments

Although these norms for sexual ethics continue to be upheld by many in the church, there can be no question that the topic of sexuality is a battlefield in the church today. Why devote so much attention to the topic of homosexuality? First, most of the debate about sexuality has been focused on the controversial topic of homosexuality. Further, the topic of homosexuality is important because it affects the lives of human beings who experience or contend with same-sex attraction and are either led toward or away from loving communion with our merciful God. Finally, the topic of homosexuality is important because it is the focus of the broader moral debate about sexual ethics, and thus it draws our attention to fundamental questions about the nature of God's revelation to us, of his claim over us and of our very understanding of our natures and callings.

Recent developments have led to a heated debate about the moral status of same-sex unions and the ordination of practicing homosexual persons. The following quotes are indicative of efforts to bring science in to move the debate along a certain path:

> Contemporary social science research [tells us] that sexual orientation, whether heterosexual, homosexual, or bisexual, is not consciously chosen by individuals but rather discovered in the process of psychosexual development and maturation. . . . The focus of moral concern should, therefore, shift to the pervasive societal fear and hatred of gay men and lesbians and the intolerance of sexual difference.[9]

> If it could be shown that homosexuality is generally a symptom of unmet emotional needs or difficulties in social adjustment, then this might point to problems in relating to God and other persons. But if that cannot gener-

---

[9]Marvin Ellison, "Homosexuality and Protestantism," in *Homosexuality and World Religions*, ed. Arlene Swidler (Valley Forge, Penn.: Trinity Press International, 1993), pp. 149-80.

ally be shown, homosexuality may be compatible with life in grace. . . . The scientific evidence is sufficient to support the contention that homosexuality is not pathological or otherwise an inversion, developmental failure, or deviant form of life as such, but is rather a human variant, one that can be healthy and whole.[10]

Expert opinion is largely agreed . . . that a sexual orientation is not, in the vast majority of cases, voluntary in the sense of a self-conscious choice. . . . If it is granted that a homosexual orientation is involuntary . . . it is unjust to present celibacy as a calling.[11]

If organic or body-chemical explanations should, however, prevail, we are reminded . . . how this would make even more indefensible moral condemnation of same-sex preference or assertions of its unnaturalness.[12]

In the chapters that follow we will discuss the scientific basis for these and other claims made by proponents for change from the traditional Christian sexual ethic. We will also discuss the formal relevance of the scientific research to the moral debate in the church. Before we examine the scientific findings and their relevance to the moral debate, we want to first discuss key issues related to research on homosexuality.

Issues Related to Research on Homosexuality

Because we want to take science seriously, we have to appreciate what science can tell us, but we must also appreciate the limitations there are to scientific methods of obtaining knowledge. Of particular concern are the limitations to the existing research on homosexuality, and so we now turn our attention to a number of issues that make the topic of homosexuality so challenging and complex.

Individual differences. The first problem that plagues research on sexual orientation generally, and on homosexuality specifically, is the diversity of persons to whom the description "homosexual" is applied. This one label, "homosexual," encompasses an enormous array of very diverse

---

[10]*Report of the Committee to Study Homosexuality to the General Council on Ministries of the United Methodist Church* (Dayton, Ohio: General Council on Ministries, 1991), pp. 27-28.

[11]Protestant Episcopal Church, "Standing Commission on Human Affairs," *Blue Book of the Episcopal Church General Convention* (New York: The Episcopal Church General Convention, 1991), pp. 199, 202.

[12]George Edwards, *Gay/Lesbian Liberation: A Biblical Perspective* (New York: Pilgrim, 1984), p. 23.

people, and the real individual differences between those many persons may be sacrificed when the generic labels "homosexual" or "gay and lesbian" are used. For example, some people experience same-sex attraction and self-identify as gay or lesbian; others identify as bisexual; still others identify as heterosexual but may experience same-sex attraction or thoughts. We have known people who identify themselves as gay or lesbian and claim to have "always been different," and others who have experimented or embraced a same-sex identity following years of heterosexual marriage and parenting. Some homosexual people behave and feel very differently from the typical pattern for their biological gender (i.e., the effeminate male or masculine female), while others do not experience themselves as different from the typical male or female (except, of course, in who they are attracted to). Labels and categories can rob real people of their uniqueness.

Essentialist-constructionist debate. Another issue related to our understanding of the research is the question of what homosexuality actually *is*. In scholarly circles today this question boils down to a debate between essentialism and social constructionism. The basic debate boils down to the issue of whether or not "homosexuality" is a "real" thing (like the species Homo sapiens) or a category that exists only at this moment in time because of our shared understanding in society (like the description "Republican" in twentieth-century America).

Essentialists argue that the term *homosexual* accurately defines a person's self or inner core or nature, so that sexual orientation is intimately intertwined with a person's true identity as a human being. As researcher Edward Laumann and his colleagues put it, "The category *homosexual* describes an aspect of the person that corresponds to some objective core or inner essence of the person."[13] We might say that the essentialist argues that "homosexual" is a real and critically important description of a person in some manner parallel to that individual being a "female" or a "human being," which are assumed to be real, enduring and universal categorizations.

Essentialists typically make one fundamental claim, and some essentialists, but not all, go on to make one or two additional claims:

---

[13]Edward O. Laumann, John H. Gagnon, Robert T. Michael and Stuart Michaels, *The Social Organization of Sexuality* (Chicago: University of Chicago Press, 1994), p. 285.

The first and most explicit claim is that homosexuality, or sexual orientation more generally, is an enduring and universal reality, an essence. . . .
Second, some (but not all) essentialists argue that this essence is ineluctra-
bly bound to the core of one's self as a particular human being. The third
claim often follows from the second: because this real essence is a part of
what properly defines the core of the person, homosexual behavior is naturally occurring, morally blameless behavior that should find expression.[14]

Acceptance of all three of these claims probably best describes the position taken by most proponents of gay-affirming morality, who would
argue that expression of that identity (same-sex behavior) is essential to
their human wholeness.

This issue often makes its way into church documents about sexuality.
The committee to study human sexuality from the Presbyterian Church
in the United States of America (PCUSA) argued in a way that relied
upon essentialist presuppositions when it framed the issue of sexual and
spiritual wholeness. In response to moralities calling for persons to
refrain from homosexual behavior, the committee said that "the church
requires that gays and lesbians deny, rather than affirm, their God-given
sexuality . . . they are expected not to 'practice' their sexuality, or in other
words, to refrain from experiencing the deep love and intimacy made
possible by God in our creation."[15] Such a claim makes sense only when
a person assumes that essentialism is true.

Social constructionists do not deny the existence of same-sex behaviors, attractions and so forth. But in contrast to the essentialists, they
argue that we have as a culture constructed two categories of people on

---

[14]Mark A. Yarhouse and Stanton L. Jones, "A Critique of Materialist Assumptions in
Research on Homosexuality," *Christian Scholar's Review* 26, no. 4 (1997): 482.

[15]Special Committee on Human Sexuality document for the Presbyterian Church (USA),
Presbyterians and Human Sexuality (Louisville, Ky.: Office of the General Assembly, 1991),
p. 54. The majority committee that wrote this report argues that "justice-love" is a necessary and sufficient standard for any moral obligation. Unfortunately, the committee
offered its own unique definitions of justice and love and neglected the relationship in
Scripture between love and obedience. As Jesus said, "If you love me, you will keep my
commandments" (Jn 14:15 NRSV). Likewise, Paul wrote, "Love is the fulfilling of the
law" (Rom 13:8-10 NRSV). We can see that "justice-love," as articulated by members of
the special committee, is a necessary but insufficient ingredient in a Christian sexual
ethic. We discuss the "justice-love" ethic in greater detail in chapter six. The reader
should know that the Presbyterian Church USA General Assembly rejected this majority
report from their study committee.

the basis of behaviors and attractions (heterosexual and homosexual). These categories are historical and cultural artifacts, like our political categorization in the United States of Democrats and Republicans, which are nonenduring. In support of their position, social constructionists might point to, for instance, the ancient tendency to categorize sexual actors more by who penetrates and who was penetrated than by gender. Most social constructionists are, nevertheless, broadly supportive of gay-affirmative moral systems and civil codes, in that our moral and civil codes are viewed as every bit as much a social construction as are our views of sexual orientation.

The essentialist view has been characterized by researcher Edward Laumann and his colleagues as the more widespread view by far at a popular level. It is also the one most likely to be a background assumption in contemporary moral debate about "homosexuality," this in spite of the fact that the constructionist view is the more likely background assumption of the scientists doing research on homosexuality. The debate between essentialists and constructionists is not a debate between Christians and non-Christians; it is a debate about what homosexuality or sexual orientation actually *is*. Neither the essentialist nor the constructionist view is intrinsically more supportive of a traditional sexual ethic. Like most essentialists, most constructionists are pro-gay, and they see sexual orientation like membership in a political party ("I am a socialist") and as a way of thinking about your identity that is shaped by socially determined thought forms and not by unchanging internal essences.

Most research is limited to male homosexuality. A third problem has been the research focus upon male homosexuals (gays), with very little in comparison being done with lesbians. Undoubtedly this bias in the research is reflective of a more general tendency of male researchers to ignore women. But it is probably also a function of the higher incidence of male homosexuality (which occurs about twice as often as for females), of the tendency when research was starting for male homosexuals to be more "out" and vocal, and recently of the explosion of AIDS in the gay (i.e., male) community, prompting research targeted at stopping the spread of the disease. Although we draw on research on both male and female homosexuals when it is available, the majority of the research we will review addresses male homosexuality, and future research will undoubtedly further our understanding of female homosexuality.

Nonrandom samples. A fourth problem is the difficulty or impossibility of obtaining a random and representative sample of homosexual individuals. This has been a problem in the research for the past forty years, and it remains a problem for researchers today. The importance of a representative sample is that it helps us generalize the findings from the study to other homosexual persons. When we fail to obtain a representative sample, we may still have important information about a real group of people, but it will be unclear as to whether the findings can be generalized to other homosexual persons who did not participate in the study. By analogy, if we did a study of the political attitudes of three thousand people who attend conservative Christian churches, we would have important information about those people that could perhaps be generalized to other conservative Christians. But since conservative Christians tend to be politically conservative, we could not justify any generalizations from our sample to the general population that includes believers and nonbelievers of all political stripes.

Replication. The best science is always science that can be replicated (that is, reliably repeated). When some physicists claimed to have achieved "cold fusion" a number of years back, the failure of other scientists to be able to duplicate their results in other labs led to the rapid discrediting of the original findings as legitimate science. We mention throughout the book that the failure to replicate findings has plagued research in this area of homosexuality. Many of the most widely known studies on genetics, for example, have failed replication by other research groups, or replication studies are in progress but have yet to be published. Unfortunately this is not often appreciated by those who debate the morality of homosexual behavior, given the human tendency is to look for ammunition to further his or her cause at the expense of acknowledging the potential value and limitations of those findings. Good science requires patience as we wait for results to be repeated by multiple researchers.

Conclusion

The debates about the morality of homosexual behavior have in recent years drawn heavily upon the findings from science. The scientific research on homosexuality is often cited very casually in these debates, especially in the study and support documents of the mainline Christian denominations. After the stem "Science says . . ." sweeping and inaccurate generalizations are often made. After such generalizations ethical conclusions are often thrown out that are only loosely tied to the supposed scientific findings.

Our core concerns in writing this book are twofold: (1) Those who attempt to draw on the authority of science in the moral debates continue to make inaccurate and improper generalizations about the primary research literature (such as "Science says it's all genetic"). (2) The logic by which the supposed findings of science are brought to bear on the moral issue is often illogical or tortured (such as "Homosexuals cannot change to heterosexuals, and therefore it is good to be gay!"). Thus we aspire to provide the reader with a solid overview of what the scientific research actually says and explore the logic of how it might or might not be relevant to the ethical debate among Christians.

We will review the scientific findings under the major headings that best describe the types of research cited, namely, (1) *prevalence of homosexuality* (chapter two: "How Prevalent Is Homosexuality?"), (2) *etiology* (another word for causation; chapter three: "What Causes Homosexuality?"), (3) *status as a mental disorder* (chapter four: "Is Homosexuality a Psychopathology?"), and (4) *efficacy of change methods* (chapter five: "Can Homosexuality Be Changed?"). Having reviewed the scientific findings on homosexuality and their formal relevance to the church's moral debate, we will then develop the traditionalist's understanding of the Christian sexual ethic (chapter six).

Our intention is to increase awareness that the actual findings on homosexuality are more complex and puzzling than is usually acknowledged and to discourage future selective or simplistic reporting of such findings. We also hope to offer the church a rearticulation of the traditional Christian sexual ethic and to offer an example for how findings from science—accurately understood—can inform our moral reasoning.

Discussion Questions

1. Before reading further, in what ways do you see scientific research being relevant to moral views of homosexual behavior? Can science ever affect our moral views?

2. In what ways are each of the three positions on the relationship of science and religion attractive, and what concerns do you have about

each (perspectivalism, imperialism and postmodern relativism)?

3. How is critical realism an alternative to perspectivalism, imperialism and postmodern relativism? What questions or concerns do you have about critical realism?

4. What are the benefits to and limits of dialogue on the topic of homosexuality? Would Christian people ever put a limit of any kind on dialogue about this matter?

5. What is your initial response to the Christian church's traditional view of sexuality and the recent developments that have been presented as a challenge to the traditional view?

2

How Prevalent
Is Homosexuality?

Even by American standards of interest-group celebrity, gay men have loomed large in the nation's consciousness, surfacing at Roseanne's side on prime time television, as superheroes in DC Comics and on Capitol Hill, where lawmakers fuss over showering habits in the barracks. . . . Here they were, about to sit down face to face with the President in the Oval Office, when a major national survey abruptly shrank their population to a tenth of what it was once touted to be.
— *TIME*, APRIL 26, 1993

*S*ince the release of the widely publicized Alfred Kinsey studies in the 1940s and 1950s, estimates of the prevalence of homosexual practice and orientation have played a central role in debates about homosexuality. The apocryphal prevalence estimate that "10% of the adult population is homosexual" appears frequently in church documents on human sexuality, as well as the larger scientific and professional literature. For example, in an article promoting gay-affirmative services for college students, the authors provide the following rationale for services:

> To accept the widely quoted estimate that 10% of the American population is gay is to conclude that on every college campus there may be many faculty, students, and staff who might benefit from a range of health services sensitively tailored to the special needs of gay men and women.[1]

There may indeed be several valid reasons to provide services to those who experience same-sex attraction, but the rationale provided here is that knowledge of this group is important because they constitute such a

---

[1] Carolyn Dillon, "Preparing College Health Professionals to Deliver Gay-Affirmative Services," *Journal of American College Health* 35 (1986): 36.

large percentage of the general population. A similar claim is made in a journal article published in the early 1990s, which began with the following rationale for providing counseling services to gay men and lesbians:

> Given that lesbians and gay men comprise 10 to 15 percent of the general population, today's psychotherapist cannot afford to be ignorant of the mental health needs specific to these groups.[2]

Here the inaccurate 10% figure is inflated to 15%! Again we want to recognize that there may be several good reasons to provide services to those who experience same-sex attraction. People who identify themselves as gay or lesbian will have unique circumstances that counselors will want to understand in order to be able to provide competent services. The stated rationale for services, however, is based on data that is inaccurate and misleading, and hence a misrepresentation of the actual prevalence of homosexuality.

Use of Research on Prevalence in Church Debates
The church is not exempt from these kinds of misrepresentations. Many church documents promoting dialogue on the moral status of homosexual behavior and the ordination of practicing homosexuals continue to reflect inaccuracies. We will discuss at the end of this chapter how prevalence rates should inform our moral reasoning, but we will first see how inflated estimates of the incidence of homosexuality are explicitly and implicitly referenced as the basis for significant changes in church teaching and practice. These inflated statistics have been used as a rationale for changing the church's teaching on the morality of homosexual behavior and for allowing the ordination of practicing homosexual clergy. Although correcting the 10% figure may not figure prominently in the moral debate, it is important to see the misuse of science and to clarify our present understanding of the prevalence of homosexuality.

Findings on prevalence rates are typically brought into the moral debate for one of two purposes. The first purpose is to directly advance a pro-gay argument. The second purpose is to make that pro-gay argument more plausible by creating a caricature of the traditionalist Christian

---

[2]Kris S. Morgan and Rebecca M. Nerison, "Homosexuality and Psychopolitics: An Historical Overview," *Psychotherapy* 30 (1993): 133.

ethic and then citing prevalence figures to refute the caricature. For example, in a debate between liberal Episcopal bishop John Spong and conservative Episcopal bishop John Howe, Spong reasserted the 10% prevalence figure, declaring that only narrow-minded conservatives would even bother to question the figure:

> If the best scientific data . . . seems to put the figure of gay and lesbian people in the world at about 10% of the population . . . then you and I need to realize that 10% is such a larger percentage that it could hardly be accidental.[3]

In other words, in a tone that seems confident in the scientific merit of his claim, Bishop Spong refers to the prevalence of homosexuality as a key issue in the moral debate. The reasoning seems to be that if the gay and lesbian population accounts for 10% of the general population, then presumably God—fill in the blank here—intended, created, sanctioned or blessed homosexuality as such.

The 10% figure can also be used in an indirect attempt to refute a conservative position (or, more accurately, a caricature of the conservative position). For example, if conservatives are portrayed as arguing that homosexuality is immoral or unnatural *because* it is rare (an argument that we have yet to actually see any conservative make), then the 10% prevalence figure may be cited in response. This is essentially an indirect argument intended to advance a pro-gay position, because if conservatives are caricatured as saying that homosexuality is immoral *because it is rare*, then 10% prevalence figures may make traditionalists look scientifically uninformed or naive. Without arguing explicitly for a pro-gay position, this approach makes the caricatured traditionalist position simply look untenable.

An example of the indirect approach is found in one denominational report,[4] which listed ten "myths" it aspired to dispel, the first being that

> gays and lesbians constitute only a small segment of the general population and are an urban phenomenon

---

[3]Debate between the Rev. John Spong and the Rt. Rev. John Howe at Virginia Protestant Episcopal Seminary, February 1992 (audiotape available from Truro Tape Ministries, 10520 Main St., Fairfax, VA 22030).

[4]The 203rd General Assembly Response to the Report of the Special Committee on Human Sexuality, *Presbyterians and Human Sexuality* (Louisville, Ky.: Office of the General Assembly, Presbyterian Church USA, 1991), p. 49.

to which the authors replied:

> Research from several sectors indicates that at least 10 percent of the American population or approximately 22 million persons are predominantly gay or lesbian.[5]

In either case—whether the 10% prevalence figure is cited to argue for the morality of homosexuality, or if it is cited to refute the claim that homosexuality is rare and therefore unnatural or immoral—the prevalence rate of homosexuality does appear to be a genuine point of discussion in the church today. The inaccurate 10% figure is often misused for one or the other reason. There is certainly a need to clarify what we know and what we do not know about the prevalence of homosexuality and homosexual behavior.

Review of the Scientific Findings

We mentioned above that the 10% figure is inextricably tied to the Kinsey studies published in the 1940s and 1950s. This figure was not publicly or widely called into question until the early 1990s. One of the first grand stage indictments of the 10% prevalence figure was a *Time* magazine article published in 1993 entitled "The Shrinking Ten Percent." The author, Priscilla Painton, referenced a major national survey where only 1% of the 3,321 men surveyed considered themselves exclusively homosexual.

The implications of this dramatically reduced prevalence figures was not lost on Painton, as the quote that introduced this chapter suggests:

> Even by American standards of interest-group celebrity, gay men have loomed large in the nation's consciousness, surfacing at Roseanne's side on prime time television, as superheroes in DC Comics and on Capitol Hill, where lawmakers fuss over showering habits in the barracks. . . . Here they were, about to sit down face to face with the President in the Oval Office, when a major national survey abruptly shrank their population to a tenth of what it was once touted to be.

Painton discusses further the relevance of the prevalence rates to the political concerns of the pro-gay movement. She quotes the reaction of Larry Kramer, cofounder of the pro-gay group ACT UP: "Bill Clinton

---

[5]Ibid., p. 49.

and Jesse Helms worry about 10% of the population. They don't worry about 1%. This will give Bill Clinton a chance to welch on promises."[6] Responding to the use of prevalence rates in advocacy for pro-gay causes, Kramer goes on to say that "the 10% figure . . . became part of our vocabulary. Democracy is all about proving you have the numbers. The more numbers you can prove you have, the more likely you'll get your due."[7] In fact, Bruce Voeller claims to have originated the 10% estimate as part of the modern gay rights campaign in the late 1970s to convince politicians and the public that "we [gays and lesbians] are everywhere." At the time Voeller was the chair of the National Gay Task Force.[8]

Setting aside the potential uses or misuses of prevalence rates, we focus now on what we actually know from the behavioral science research about the prevalence rates of homosexuality and homosexual behavior. We begin with a critique of the research that originated the 10% figure: The Alfred Kinsey studies.

Alfred Kinsey was a biologist (an entomologist—a scientist who studies insects—to be specific) at the University of Indiana who, in the 1940s and 1950s, chose to turn his scientific interest to the topic of human sexuality. Kinsey interviewed what were at that time *huge* samples of people and asked them what were, at that time, astonishingly frank and detailed questions about their sexual behavior. The subsequent publication of his major books was a public scandal in its own right. The books, written in excruciating, dry and arithmetical detail, were surprise bestsellers and the focus of much public debate.

The 10% figure is usually attributed to the Kinsey studies of males.[9] What many people may not know is that Kinsey *never* reported that "10% of the population is homosexual," as is often suggested in popular reports or discussions. Kinsey actually reported a range of different statistics on homosexual behavior:

☐ that 4% of white males were exclusively homosexual throughout their

[6]Patricia Painton, "The Shrinking Ten Percent," *Time,* April 26, 1993, p. 27.
[7]Ibid.
[8]Edward O. Laumann, John H. Gagnon, Robert T. Michael and Stuart Michaels, *The Social Organization of Sexuality* (Chicago: University of Chicago Press, 1994), p. 289.
[9]Alfred C. Kinsey, Wardell B. Pomeroy and Clyde E. Martin, *Sexual Behavior in the Human Male* (Philadelphia: Saunders, 1948).

lives after adolescence

☐ that a total of 10% of white males were "more or less" exclusively homosexual during at least a three-year period between the ages of 16 and 55

☐ that 37% of males experience at least some homosexual behavior to the point of orgasm between adolescence and adulthood

☐ that 50% of males have neither attraction to nor the experience of homosexual behavior

☐ that 25% had "more than incidental" homosexual experience "or reactions" between adolescence and adulthood[10]

Kinsey also consistently reported in his later study of female sexuality that female homosexuality appeared to occur at about half the rate of male homosexuality.[11]

So the first thing to note about Kinsey's "findings" is that the "10% of the population is homosexual" claim *is not one that Kinsey ever made.*

Further, researchers rarely discuss just how deeply flawed Kinsey's data appear to be. For a study such as Kinsey's to produce data from which we could generalize to the whole population, the sample under study would have to be roughly representative of that general population. If you want to study the healthiness of the American population, for instance, you would not do most of your interviews in either a health club (which would create a positive bias) or a hospital (which would create a negative bias)! But Kinsey seems to have ignored the need to keep his sample reflective of the American population. It appears as though Kinsey's sample of males was skewed because he oversampled a variety of groups (a group is oversampled when a higher percentage of group members are included in a study than there are members of those groups in the general population). And curiously, every example of oversampling appears to have increased the likelihood of finding a higher incidence of nontraditional sexual practices. At a time when many fewer people went to college, Kinsey oversampled college graduates (who were found by Kinsey to be more likely to have engaged in "unusual" sexual practices than the noncollege sample). He included a higher percentage

---

[10]Ibid., pp. 650-51.

[11]Alfred C. Kinsey, Wardell B. Pomeroy, Clyde E. Martin and Paul H. Gebhard, *Sexual Behavior in the Human Female* (Philadelphia: Saunders, 1953).

of Protestants and fewer Catholics than was representative of the population (and, not coincidentally, Catholics were less likely to have engaged in "unusual" sexual practices).

But two sample distortions are the most shocking: First, Kinsey drastically oversampled prison inmates.[12] Adding insult to injury, when he gained access to interviews with prison populations, he especially sought interviews with sex offenders, men imprisoned for such crimes as rape, pederasty (child molestation) and sodomy (homosexual behavior). Kinsey's focus on prison populations also sheds light on the finding of the frequency with which some men spent at least three years of their life exclusively engaged in homosexual behavior—what other options are there for men in prison? Second, Kinsey drastically oversampled members of gay-affirming organizations. A recent study reviewed Kinsey's methodology and commented, "Kinsey roamed far and wide in selecting his subjects. . . . Kinsey also purposefully recruited subjects for his research from homosexual friendship and acquaintance networks in big cities."[13] This is obviously not the type of methodology a person would implement if he or she were trying to get a representative outlook on the sexual behavior of the general population.

So *both* figures—the "4% exclusively homosexual throughout their lives" figure and the "10% exclusively homosexual during a three-year period" figure—are probably inflated due to oversampling from a subject pool that is more likely to engage in same-sex behavior to begin with. It has been amazing to see how these figures have persisted in contemporary discussions, despite the major problems with their accuracy and credibility.

Much more credible studies that address the prevalence rate of homosexuality have been published in recent years. These studies consistently have found remarkably lower prevalence rates than those reported by Kinsey and promoted by others (including those promoting change in the church).

Before we dive into the actual numbers, we must begin with a sketch

---

[12] These problems are discussed in detail in Judith A. Reisman and Edward W. Eichel, Albert H. Hobbs and J. Gordon Muir, *Kinsey, Sex, and Fraud: The Indoctrination of a People* (Lafayette, La.: Huntington House, 1990).

[13] Laumann et al., *Social Organization*, p. 289.

of the complexity of defining homosexuality. You have probably begun to ponder this already as you read through the differing statistics offered by Kinsey relevant to homosexuality. The seemingly simple question "How many people are homosexual?" ceases to be simple when we stop to define what we mean by the word homosexual. Who counts as a homosexual? Does the man who says "I am a homosexual" but who is married to a woman and only engages in homosexual sex once in a while in anonymous encounters count? Does the woman who was married for fifteen years, had three children, and then declared herself a lesbian? Does the seventeen-year-old man who fantasizes about sex with both men and women but has never actually had sex?

Prevalence can be defined in different ways. The studies we will cite often utilize several different definitions or indices of prevalence, including when a respondent (1) identifies his or her sexual orientation, (2) reports experiencing same-sex attraction and (3) identifies occurrences of same-sex behavior. The most commonly cited measure of sexual orientation appears to be self-identification of a person's sexual orientation (that is, identifying himself or herself as heterosexual, homosexual or bisexual), even though such a self-identification can mean different things to different people.

Prevalence estimates of homosexuality based on self-identification of a person's own sexual orientation range from 2% to 4%. The study that best meets the widest array of scientific standards for accuracy and representativeness is a large national survey of nearly 5,000 respondents that was carefully constructed to accurately represent the population of the United States and published by Edward Laumann and his colleagues. The Laumann study found that 2.0% of men and 0.9% of women identified themselves as homosexual, and an additional 0.8% of men and 0.5% of women identified themselves as bisexual.[14] They also asked about the degree to which those responding to the interview were attracted to members of the same sex. They found that 6.2% of men and 4.4% of women reported feeling attracted to members of the same sex, and this was independent of whether they experienced heterosexual attraction. Similarly, Laumann and his colleagues asked about the degree to which those responding to the interview found the idea of sex with

---

[14]Ibid., chap. 8.

someone of their same gender appealing and found that 4.5% of men and 5.6% of women said they found this idea appealing.

Gay sociologist Joseph Harry found similar results in another carefully designed and executed study.[15] He reported that 2.4% of men surveyed described themselves as homosexual. Interestingly, Harry reported the additional statistic that up to 5.7% of those surveyed could be described as homosexual *if (IF!)* all those who described themselves as bisexual *and* all those who refused to answer the question about sexual orientation were also classified as homosexual. This is a *very questionable* set of categorizations—while some people who are basically homosexual but who are conflicted or confused about their desires may call themselves bisexual in response to survey questions, it seems certain that not all who describe themselves as bisexual are really homosexual, and why should that small number who refuse to answer the question all be assumed to be homosexual? However, this does raise a question that is asked of every survey: Are respondents being honest and forthright with researchers when they provide answers to these kinds of questions? Scientists are limited here by the nature of survey instruments. Researchers can really only go with those answers people provide. At the same time, researchers often wonder what answers would have been provided by those who failed to answer specific questions. However, Harry's dubious assumption that those who did not respond were probably homosexual is better characterized as wishful thinking rather than an empirical finding on prevalence.

Poorly designed surveys can produce misleading results, and even well-designed surveys can be interpreted incorrectly. For example, a recent report of a major survey[16] presented the highly provocative findings that 20.8% of males and 17.8% of females in the United States (and similar rates for the United Kingdom and France) experience either sexual attraction toward or sexual behavior with persons of the same gender. Some news reports of this study reported that it had found that 20% of the population was homosexual.

---

[15] Joseph Harry, "A Probability Sample of Gay Males," *Journal of Homosexuality* 19 (1990): 89-104.

[16] Randall L. Sell, James A. Wells and David Wypij, "The Prevalence of Homosexual Behavior and Attraction in the United States, the United Kingdom, and France: Results of National Population-Based Samples," *Archives of Sexual Behavior* 24 (1995): 235-48.

We believe that these are inflated estimates of the frequency of homosexual attraction. The inflated estimates are due to poor survey design. The researchers forced those heterosexuals who participated in the survey to choose between the following two items:

1. "I have absolutely never felt any sexual attraction toward someone of my own sex."

or

2. "I have felt attracted toward someone of my own sex but never had any sexual contact with anyone."

It would appear that this question forced any heterosexual who had ever felt even the most vague attraction to a person of the same gender to endorse the latter item, which would account for the inflated rates of same-gender attraction. This is especially misleading when we consider that some researchers[17] have found that as many as 20% of adolescents have at some point felt some kind of arousal to homosexual thoughts (presumably because of the diffuse nature of sexual attraction in adolescence, where males in particular can find themselves aroused by a variety of stimuli). Because of the way in which the survey question was worded, a person who reluctantly rejected the first choice ("I guess I can not say that I have absolutely never felt any sexual attraction toward someone of my own sex") is suddenly interpreted (misinterpreted) as a person who "feels" (as in "commonly feels," "regularly feels," "often feels") homosexual attraction. But a few passing feelings of attraction at some point in a person's past hardly qualify him or her as a person who feels stable, same-gender attraction, which is what most people think of when they think of homosexuality or a homosexual person.

Studies of the prevalence of homosexuality where homosexuality is defined as same-sex *behavior* yield the lowest estimates of all of the various estimates of prevalence. Table 2.1 is organized around major prevalence findings of same-sex sexual behavior as reported from national surveys, which are probably the most representative surveys available. As was mentioned above, most researchers described their findings as on the lower end of estimates about prevalence given the general reluctance

---

[17]See Nathaniel McConaghy's discussion of this in *Sexual Behavior: Problems and Management* (New York: Plenum, 1993), pp. 101-8.

on the part of those who respond to surveys to admit to stigmatized behavior. In other words, they usually characterize their estimates as minimal estimates of prevalence, descriptions of the lowest prevalence estimate that is credible.

As we consider the research in table 2.1, numerous findings are striking. One is the gap between the approximately 1% of males who engaged exclusively in same-sex behavior in the past year and the 1.1% to 2.7% who experienced any same-sex behavior in the past year. It would appear that for every one man who is exclusively homosexual, there is another who engages in both homosexual *and* heterosexual behavior in a given year. This gap may be explained in part by the separate and surprising finding that 42% of those who identified themselves as gay or bisexual men in Harry's national survey were married to women.[18] The low frequency of male lifetime homosexual experience in table 2.1 compared to Kinsey's estimate of 37%, and the impossibility of his 10% estimate of three-year exclusive male homosexual experience, are both remarkable.

The "myth" we mentioned above—that "gays and lesbians constitute only a small segment of the general population and are an urban phenomenon"—may not be a myth after all. The percentage of those who identify themselves as gay or lesbian or who engage in same-sex behavior is certainly lower than is often publicized. Curiously, it is precisely because homosexuality is by and large an urban phenomenon that it may *seem* to some that 10% of the population is gay. The "urban phenomenon" could be the result of migration of gay and lesbian persons to urban settings, or it could be a reflection of a disinhibited subculture in an urban setting where there is a shared sense of support and affirmation.[19] There are probably sections of many major urban centers where homosexual persons live in greater numbers and thus feel greater freedom to openly manifest their homosexual preferences; anyone who lives in or visits such an area is going to be struck by how it appears that a substantial part of the population is homosexual.

---

[18]Harry, "Probability Sample."
[19]See Laumann et al., *Social Organization*, pp. 306-9.

Study	Exclusive Same-Gender Sex in Last ___ Years	Occurrence of Same-Gender Sex in Last Year	Occurrence Last ___ Years	Occurrence Since Adulthood (Age ___)	Occurrence Since Puberty (or Lifetime)
Billy et al. (1993) Males only	1.1% in last 10 years		2.3% in last 10 years		
Fay et al. (1989) Males only		1.6-2.0%		6.7% since age 19 (3.3% occasionally or fairly often)	20.3%
Laumann et al. (1994) Males		2.7%	4.1% in last five years	4.9% since age 18	9.1%
Laumann et al. (1994) Females		1.3%	2.2% in last five years	4.1% since age 18	4.3%
Rogers & Turner (1991) Males only		Study 1: 1.9% Study 2: 1.2% Study 3: 2.4% Study 4: 2.0%		All since 18 Study 1: 4.8% Study 2: 4.9% Study 3: N/A Study 4: 6.7%	
Sell et al. (1995) Males	Last 5 years: US-0.82% UK-1.15% Fr.-0.72%		Last 5 years: US-5.42% UK-3.51% Fr.-9.94%		

Study				
Sell et al. (1995) Females	Last 5 years: US-0.27% UK-0.54% Fr.-0.14%		Last 5 years: US-2.96% UK-1.54% Fr.-3.02%	
Spira et al. (1993) Males only (France)	1.1%			4.1%
Stall et al. (1990) Males only	0.8% in last five years	1.4% in last five years		
Wellings et al. (1994) Males (Britain)	1.1%			6.1%
Wellings et al. (1994) Female (Britain)	0.4%			3.4%

Table 2.1. Frequency reports of same-gender sexual behavior over various time periods from major national probability survey studies. The citations for the specific studies are: John O. Billy, Koray Tanfer, William R. Grady and Daniel H. Klepinger, "The Sexual Behavior of Men in the United States," *Family Planning Perspectives* 25 (1993): 52-61; Robert Fay, Charles Turner, Albert Klassen and John Gagnon, "Prevalence and Patterns of Same-Gender Sexual Contact Among Men," *Science* 243 (1989): 338-48; Laumann et al., *The Social Organization*; Randall L. Sell, James A. Wells and David Wypij, "The Prevalence of Homosexual Behavior and Attraction in the United States, the United Kingdom, and France: Results of National Population-Based Samples," *Archive of Sexual Behavior* 24 (1995): 235-48; Susan M. Rogers and Charles F. Turner, "Male-Male Sexual Contact in the U.S.A.: Findings from Five Sample Surveys, 1970-1990," *Journal of Sex Research* 28 (1991): 491-519; Spira et al., cited in Laumann et al., *The Social Organization*; Ron Stall, John Gagnon, Thomas Coates, Joseph Catania and James Wiley, "Prevalence of Men Who Have Sex with Men in the United States," in Joseph Catania (chairperson), *Results from the First National AIDS Behavioral Survey*, symposium presented at the convention of the American Psychological Association, San Francisco (August 1990); Kaye Wellings, Julia Field, Anne Johnson and Jane Wadsworth, *Sexual Behavior in Britain: The National Survey of Sexual Attitudes and Lifestyles* (New York: Penguin, 1994). Note that the Rogers and Turner study is a composite report of four national probability surveys, and that the Sell et al. study reports separately on U.S., United Kingdom and French samples.

One study[20] has attempted to account for this. A sample of males in major urban settings (which is obviously not representative of the country at large) was compared to a national sample. The researchers reported that the percentages of men who had had sex only with other males in the last five years rose from 1.4% (in the national sample) to 3.7% (in the urban sample), with an additional 2.0% of men in the urban setting having had sex with both men and women in the last five years.

Similarly, Laumann[21] and his colleagues examined respondents who lived in the twelve major urban centers of the United States and found that those who identified themselves as gay, lesbian or bisexual rose to 9.2% of men and 2.6% of women, with reports of any same-sex behavior since puberty increasing to 15.8% of men and 4.6% of women. In other words, research appears to support the perception that those who identify themselves as homosexual or who engage in homosexual behavior are more likely to be found in urban settings.

Conclusion on Prevalence

As we conclude this review of the research, we can accurately say, based on the scientific findings available to date, that the rate of homosexuality as a stable life orientation in our culture is certainly not 10%. There is good evidence to suggest that less than 3%, and perhaps less than 2%, of males are homosexually active in a given year. The rate of males who engage in sustained homosexual practice over a significant period of adult life is probably less than 5% of the male population. The rate of men who manifest a sustained and exclusive commitment to homosexual practice is certainly less than 3%.

Female homosexuality has not been studied as extensively and continues to be estimated at approximately half or less than the male rates. Female homosexuality appears to characterize less than 2% of the female population. So when males and females are combined, homosexuality almost certainly characterizes less than 3% of the population, and the correct percentage combining men and women might be lower than even 2%.

---

[20]Ron Stall, John Gagnon, Thomas Coates, Joseph Catania and James Wiley, "Prevalence of Men Who Have Sex with Men in the United States," in J. Catania (chairperson), *Results from the First National AIDS Behavioral Survey* (symposium presented at the convention of the American Psychological Association, San Francisco, August 1990).

[21]Laumann et al., *Social Organization*, chap. 8.

Formal Relevance of Research to the Moral Debate

What is the formal or logical relevance of the prevalence rates of homosexuality and homosexual behavior to the contemporary moral debate in the church? What weight should be given to prevalence rates when considering the morality of homosexual behavior? Does it matter that homosexuality appears to characterize about 2-3% of the population? Would the church's moral position change if these figures were to rise dramatically?

Whether homosexual behavior is rare or common should not play a major role in whether we view homosexual behavior as immoral. We can think of no compelling rationale for why the prevalence of a particular behavior should be directly related to whether that behavior is moral. Some behaviors that Christians deem to be sins are common, such as greed, pride and lust. Many people throughout history have struggled with these vices and the behaviors that express those vices across relationships. The fact that these are common experiences does not detract from the fact that the church identifies these behaviors as wrong or immoral. Other behaviors are quite rare. For example, cannibalism, necrophilia (sexual attraction to dead bodies) and pedophilia (sexual attraction to children) are rare and are considered wrong or immoral. The fact that pedophilia is rare does not make it immoral. If "rareness" made something immoral, then the heights of virtue that are so infrequently seen among us would also have to be classed as immoral. Pedophilia and similar distortions are determined to be immoral based on considerations beyond the claim that they are rare. So there does not appear to be an obvious reason to assume that the prevalence of a behavior has a direct bearing on whether it is a sin or moral concern.

To apply this understanding to the issue of homosexuality, the prevalence of same-sex attraction or homosexual behavior has no obvious or clear relevance to the church's view of its moral status. Patterns that are common or uncommon may be immoral or moral. Although the debate about the morality of homosexual behavior can be informed by scientific findings such as the prevalence of homosexuality and homosexual behavior, the difficult, complicated moral questions cannot be answered by simply citing research on the prevalence of the behavior.

Having said this, it is important to remember that inflated prevalence rates are often cited in working documents intended to change the Christian's moral stance on homosexuality and the ordination of practicing homosexual clergy. Just as there is no reason to deem homosexual behavior immoral because it is rare, there is no reason to view it as morally neutral or as a moral good because of the misperception that it is more common than it is.

Summary

☐ Proponents for change offer two types of arguments. The first is that homosexuality is common and therefore should not be viewed as a moral concern in and of itself. The second argument is to caricature traditionalists as saying that homosexuality is immoral *because it is rare*. By framing the debate in this way, scientific research on higher prevalence rates will make the caricature of the traditionalist seem untenable.

☐ The infamous "10% of the population is gay" pronouncement has been consistently shown to be based on a misinterpretation of deeply flawed research published by Kinsey.

☐ More recent and more credible studies suggest that less than 3%, and perhaps less than 2%, of males are homosexually active in a given year.

☐ Probably fewer than 5% of the adult male population engage in sustained homosexual practice over a significant period of adult life.

☐ Female homosexuality is estimated at approximately half or less than the male rates and appears to characterize less than 2% of the female population.

☐ Combining males and females, homosexuality almost certainly characterizes less than 3% (and perhaps less than 2%) of the population.

Discussion Questions

1. What was your impression of the prevalence of homosexuality prior to reading this chapter? Where did you learn about the prevalence of homosexuality?

2. In what ways have lowered prevalence rates increased sympathy for the pro-gay movement?

3. What explanation might you give for research that suggests that homosexuality may be more common in urban rather than rural or suburban settings?

4. What weight should be given to the prevalence rates of homosexuality or homosexual behavior in the present moral debates in the church?

3

What Causes Homosexuality?

Genes are hardware . . . the data of life's experiences are processed through the sexual
software into the circuits of identity. I suspect the sexual software is a mixture of both
genes and environment, in much the same way the software of a computer is a mixture
of what's installed at the factory and what's added by the user.
— PETER COPELAND AND DEAN HAMER,
THE SCIENCE OF DESIRE

*O*ne of the most common questions we are asked by people in the
church, people in the broader society, homosexuals themselves, and parents and friends of homosexual persons is,
What causes homosexuality? Admittedly, some ask the
question with a sneer; they are committed to the view that it is a self-
consciously chosen sexual preference and an immoral one at that.
"They're homosexual because they choose to be," they say. Others ask
the same question and have the same sneer because they believe homosexuality is caused by one factor (whatever that may be); they are
ready to reject research as irrelevant to their experiences or the experiences of others. Still others ask, "What causes homosexuality?" out of
genuine desire to know the truth and, just as important, out of genuine
care for the well-being of others.

In any case, the question is being asked anew with special intensity
because of the general belief that the answer has important implications
for the church debates about the morality of homosexuality. What are
some of the ways in which scientific evidence about the causes of homosexuality is cropping up in the church debates?

Use of Research on the Origins of Homosexuality in Church Debates
Assumptions about the causes of homosexuality receive a great deal of
attention in the written and verbal debates about the moral status of
same-sex behavior. In the many church documents on sexuality and sexual ethics, casual references are made to "what science tells us" and many
claims about morality follow.

In the previous chapter we mentioned how findings from science are
often brought into the moral debate about homosexuality in two distinct
ways. They are sometimes used to directly advance the argument that *if*
it can be established that homosexuality is *caused* rather than *chosen*, then
homosexuality cannot be immoral. We will formally evaluate the logic of
this claim at the end of this chapter. The second approach, an indirect
one, is more common, however. This strategy is seen when pro-gay arguments are advanced by exaggerating or caricaturing the traditionalist's
perspective. When the caricature is rejected on the basis of the supposed
findings of science, the traditional position is weakened.

The most common and important caricature is that the traditional
view is built on the belief that all experiences and expressions of homosexuality are freely chosen, that they are deliberate and willful. Although
we will turn to the church documents in a moment, a good example of
this actually appeared in a *Time* magazine article entitled "Search for a
Gay Gene." The writer of the article notes that

> gays and lesbians welcome [research on genetics] because it supports what
> most of them have long felt: that homosexuality is an innate characteristic,
> like skin color, rather than a *perverse life-style choice, as conservative moralists
> contend.* And if that is true, then gays deserve legal protection similar to the
> laws that prohibit racial discrimination.[1]

Without even looking at the quality of the genetic research, the writer
has presented the reader with an *either-or* view of the homosexuality
debate: homosexuality is *either* an innate characteristic (deserving legal
protection and, by implication, full acceptance) *or* a perverse lifestyle
choice. Since "conservative moralists" are caricatured as saying that
homosexuality is a "perverse life-style choice," then any research that
appears to support a genetic hypothesis for homosexuality will make any

---

[1] Larry Thompson, "Search for a Gay Gene," *Time*, June 12, 1995, p. 61, emphasis added.

conservative position (that is, any position that fails to be pro-gay) look scientifically naive, uninformed and, most importantly, false.

Among pro-gay advocates affiliated with the church, perhaps the most outspoken person in this regard is liberal Episcopal bishop John Spong. In a recent book with the ominous title *Why Christianity Must Change or Die*, Bishop Spong draws direct implications for the moral debate from the supposed findings of science:

> When a homosexual orientation is revealed by the development of the science of the brain and its neurochemical processes to be a normal part of the sexual spectrum of human life, a given and not a chosen way of life, then it becomes inhuman to use a person's sexual orientation as the basis for a continuing prejudice. Therefore, the kind of judgment that compromises the worth and well-being of a homosexual person or places limits on the opportunities of that person becomes the activity of ignorance.[2]

Spong claims that science has settled several issues. First, he claims that science tells us that homosexuality is a "normal part of the sexual spectrum of human life." Second, he claims that the scientific findings are directly relevant to the moral debate. Third, he claims that science somehow then teaches us that there should not be any "limits on the opportunities" of homosexual persons, which, for Spong, includes the sanctioning of same-sex unions and the ordination of practicing homosexual persons. Finally, he declares that any resistance to his radical advocacy for change is steeped in ignorance. Spong not only sets up a series of stark either-or choices, with science on the side of the proponents for change of our moral standards, but he caricatures traditionalists or conservatives by placing them in the unenviable position of having to refute what science apparently teaches with absolute clarity.

The same line of reasoning appears in church documents promoting the view that homosexual behavior is moral. For example, the leader's manual[3] for a recent Episcopal "sexuality dialogue" process presents four views on the morality of homosexuality. The first position, the one that is

---

[2]John Shelby Spong, *Why Christianity Must Change or Die: A Bishop Speaks to Believers in Exile* (San Francisco: HarperSanFrancisco, 1998), pp. 161-62.

[3]Protestant Episcopal Church, "Standing Commission on Human Affairs," in *Blue Book of the Episcopal Church General Convention* (The Episcopal Church General Convention, 1991), p. 199.

supposed to represent the traditional position, is a partial caricature: "All homosexual acts are sin, first, because they violate the strictures of Scripture and, second, because they are a willful perversion of the natural order."[4] It is certainly true that most conservatives ground their opposition to changing Christian morality in the clear teaching of Scripture. The important phrase here, though, is "willful perversion." The implication seems to be that traditionalists must believe that all homosexuals have willfully chosen to be perverted. If traditionalists can be caricatured as saying that homosexuality is immoral because it is a "willful perversion," then any evidence that suggests that homosexuality is neither "willful" nor a "perversion" will undermine the traditionalist's credibility. If science can show that a homosexual orientation is not chosen but is a "given" in a person's life, then the traditionalist loses credibility for arguing that homosexuality is always a willful perversion.

Just as *willfulness* is an important word, so too is the word *perversion*, which brings to mind whether homosexuality is *natural*. If the traditionalist can be presented as arguing that homosexuality is immoral *because* it is a perversion, then scientific evidence that suggests homosexuality is natural will appear to defeat the traditionalist's position. Timothy Sedgwick, working as a member of a task force addressing human sexuality for the Episcopal church, argues as follows:

> Studies from the natural sciences suggest that homosexuality is an outcome of both biological and social factors. Homosexuality is not simply a matter of arrested development but a variable form of sexual identity in animals and human beings.[5]

Sedgwick appeals to science to support his view that homosexuality is natural. By vague reference to "studies from the natural sciences," Sedgwick has put forth an argument that challenges the caricature of the traditionalist. If indeed homosexuality is immoral *because* it is unnatural, then evidence from science that it is natural will challenge the traditionalists' position.

In an edited volume promoting church dialogue, John McNeil argues

---

[4]Ibid., p. 202.

[5]Timothy Sedgwick, "Christian Ethics and Human Sexuality: Mapping the Conversation," in *Continuing the Dialogues: Sexuality: A Divine Gift* (Task Force on Human Sexuality, Education for Mission and Ministry Unit: The Episcopal Church, New York, 1988), p. 11.

that scientific findings regarding the origins of homosexuality invalidate traditionalists' concerns for morality and concomitant call for celibacy:

> Some churches, in the face of psychological evidence that sexual orientation is not freely chosen, have begun to distinguish between homosexual orientation—which they agree, is not morally culpable—and homosexual activity, which is always morally wrong insofar as it is freely chosen. This compromise is intrinsically unstable. . . . Only a sadistic God would create hundreds of thousands of humans to be inherently homosexual and then deny them the right to sexual intimacy."[6]

A similar argument is advanced by Sylvia Thorson-Smith in a book promoting the morality of homosexual behavior and the ordination of practicing homosexuals. She cites a letter that states, "Recent developments in behavioral science suggest that physical conditions determine sexual orientation. Although the evidence is still inconclusive, if the recent discoveries prove accurate, the individual does not have the free choice that is an essential to sinful behavior."[7]

We want to briefly address the arguments raised by David Myers in a recent book that Stan helped to edit[8] that further exemplify the types of problems noted above. Myers suggests that the "accumulating [scientific] evidence," along with the experiences of gays and lesbians, should force a reexamination of the presumption that "homosexuality is a lifestyle choice."[9] He argues that since "it becomes difficult to avoid the conclusion that sexual orientation appears not to be a choice" then this "leaves one free to regard homosexuality as . . . a natural part of human diversity."[10] His clear implication, just as we discussed above, appears to be that the conceptualization of homosexuality as a lifestyle choice is

---

[6] John J. McNeil, "Homosexuality: Challenging the Church to Grow," in *Homosexuality in the Church*, ed. Jeffrey S. Siker (Louisville, Ky.: Westminster John Knox, 1994), p. 53.

[7] A letter from William P. Thompson to Vernon B. Van Bruggen, October 15, 1993, cited in Sylvia Thorson-Smith, *Reconciling the Broken Silence: The Church in Dialogue on Gay and Lesbian Issues* (Louisville, Ky.: Christian Education Program Area of the Congregational Ministry Division, Presbyterian Church USA., 1993), p. 30.

[8] David G. Myers, "A Levels-of-Explanation View," in *Psychology & Christianity: Four Views*, ed. Eric L. Johnson and Stanton L. Jones (Downers Grove, Ill.: InterVarsity Press, 2000), pp. 54-83.

[9] Ibid., p. 79.

[10] Ibid.

essential to seeing homosexual behavior as a sin.

Myers summarizes the accumulating evidence he has in mind in two assertions related to causation: "There is no known parental or psychological influence on sexual orientation" and "Biological factors are looking more and more important."[11] As we will discuss below, we would argue that both of these statements are wrong; evidence supporting the role of familial and psychological factors in homosexual causation is out there even if it is no longer in vogue and is being actively ignored by writers such as Myers, and the evidence for biological variables is contested and conflicting (and even, in the case of the latest genetics study discussed below, shrinking).

The appeals to science certainly raise several questions for those in the church who want to take science seriously and who view homosexuality as missing the mark of what God intends for people. Continuing with our standard format, we will first answer the question, What does the research on the origins of homosexuality actually show? and then turn to the equally important question, What is the formal relevance of this research to the moral debate within the church?

Review of the Scientific Findings

The origins of homosexuality are not clearly understood by scientists, and the topic is the subject of hot debate. Theories and empirical findings, which often contrast sharply, abound. The theories about the etiology of homosexuality fall into two very large categories: theories that point to nature (that is, biological variables) and theories that point to nurture (that is, the influence of experience, psychological variables). Many psychological theories look at the parent-child relationship, early childhood development, early homosexual experiences and childhood sexual abuse.

We will look at the evidence for the psychological theories first, but let us begin by looking at some data that is claimed by those on both sides of the nature-nurture debate. There is general agreement that childhood manifestations of gender nonconformity (such as a boy's interest in girls' company, toys, play, clothing and so on) appear to predispose the boy to adult homosexuality. For example, the official manual used by psychiatrists and psychologists to diagnose mental disorders states that

---

[11]Ibid.

by late adolescence or adulthood, about three-quarters of boys who had a childhood history of Gender Identity Disorder report a homosexual or bisexual orientation.[12]

Gender Identity Disorder is a psychiatric condition characterized by extreme levels of gender nonconformity. A child manifesting this condition will tend to insist that he or she is of the opposite gender (the biological male who says he is or wants to be a girl), cross-dress in clothing of the other sex and show a strong interest in stereotypical games of the opposite sex. The child will also be uncomfortable with his or her sex or gender role.

Gender Identity Disorder is very unusual; what about less extreme manifestations? Researchers recently conducted a large analysis of the research on the relationship between sex-typed behaviors and sexual orientation. They concluded that "for both men and women, research has firmly established that homosexual subjects recall substantially more cross-sex-typed behavior in childhood than do heterosexual subjects."[13] In other words, the best research to date suggests a relationship between homosexuality in adulthood and gender nonconformity in childhood.

Theories abound as to what causes such gender nonconformity and the later occurrence of homosexuality. Scientists who emphasize nature (that is, biological variables) argue that such early traits must indicate the powerful presence of biological forces. Those who emphasize nurture (that is, the influence of experiences) argue that powerful psychological forces are at work shaping and molding the child from the day of birth. All agree that gender nonconforming children—effeminate males and masculine females—are more likely to grow up into homosexuals, but there the agreement ends. We will touch on this topic again in the sections below. This gives the reader a brief foretaste of the kinds of controversies and complexities we will be reviewing.

---

[12]American Psychiatric Association, *Diagnostic and Statistical Manual of Mental Disorders, Fourth Edition* (Washington, D.C.: American Psychiatric Association, 1994), p. 536.

[13]J. Michael Bailey, and Kenneth J. Zucker, "Childhood Sex-Typed Behavior and Sexual Orientation: A Conceptual Analysis and Quantitative Review," *Developmental Psychology* 31 (1995): 49. The mean effect size for men was 1.31, *SD* = 0.43; the mean effect size for women was 0.96, *SD* = 0.35.

Psychological/Environmental Theories

Psychoanalytic theory. Among psychological theories, the psychoanalytic theory has by far been the most prominent theory for the origins of homosexuality. The "classic" psychoanalytic theory of the "cause" of male homosexuality implicates a close-binding mother and a rejecting, absent or detached father. At the most basic level the idea is that male homosexuality is caused by the failure of normal development of a secure male identity. In other words, the young boy, consciously and unconsciously, patterns his developing personality after that of his father, and this includes his father's pattern of being attracted to women. In the normal course of development the young boy "identifies" with a beloved father and is encouraged and supported in that identification by a loving mother. If a father is unavailable (either in reality or emotionally) or is an extremely undesirable figure, male identification is challenged. But the mother is important too. If the mother is threatened by the changes in the offing to her close relationship with her son, she can undermine male identification by "poisoning" the father-son relationship (through criticism of the father or of men in general, for instance) or by working to make her relationship with the boy so powerful that separation from her is impossible for the young boy. The result (according to this theory)? A young man with a compromised sense of secure "maleness" and the resulting erotic attraction toward maleness.

Most of the research supporting the psychoanalytic theory was published in the 1960s, 1970s and mid-1980s (with a shift in focus, as we shall see, toward research on biological theories in the late 1980s and 1990s). Research in support of the psychoanalytic theory includes work by Irving Bieber and his colleagues,[14] where 106 male homosexuals were compared with 100 male heterosexuals. Mothers of homosexuals were reported to have enmeshed, seductive relationships with their sons, while fathers were more commonly reported to be distant, detached or rejecting. This data was based on psychoanalysts' recollections of patients'

---

[14]Irving Bieber, Harvey J. Dain, Paul R. Dince, Marvin G. Drellich, Henry G. Grand, Ralph H. Gundlach, Malvina W. Kremer, Alfred H. Rifkin, Cornelia B. Wilbur and Toby B. Bieber, *Homosexuality: A Psychoanalytic Study of Male Homosexuals* (New York: Basic Books, 1962).

early childhood experiences. It is thus bitterly disputed by those who do not accept the theory behind it. Critics charge that the psychoanalysts gathering this "data" were already committed to their theory and then went out and found what they were determined to find and biased toward.

There have been attempts to meet these criticisms. A few years after Bieber, Evans[15] published a study that replicated the Bieber study. This second study was of 42 homosexual males and 142 heterosexual males. Evans reported very similar results, including poor parental relationships during childhood.[16] The major improvement over the Bieber study was that the findings reported by Evans were based on *self-report of homosexuals who had never sought therapy.*

Additional research in support of the role of familial variables includes the famous Bell, Weinberg and Hammersmith[17] study of approximately 1,500 homosexuals. In this study the estimate of the mother's influence on a son's homosexual development was weak, so much so that it is sometimes thought of as the study that discredited the psychoanalytic

---

[15]Ray B. Evans, "Childhood Parental Relationships of Homosexual Men," *Journal of Consulting and Clinical Psychology* 33 (1969): 129-35.

[16]However, only 28% of the homosexuals surveyed had the *same combination* of mother-son and father-son relationship observed in the Bieber study, and 11% of the control group had that combination. As these findings suggest, some studies present a different picture of the parent-child relationship, although most point to poor parent-child relationships of some kind. In some research, mothers were more dominant than fathers; other studies suggest that mothers were not close-binding but that homosexual males had poor relationships with their father. Still some studies do not point to any one consistent parent-child dynamic that is consistent across homosexual persons. See Eva Bene, "On the Genesis of Male Homosexuality: An Attempt at Clarifying the Role of the Parents," *British Journal of Psychiatry* 111 (1965): 803-13; Walter G. Stephan, "Parental Relationships and Early Social Experience of Activist Male Homosexuals and Male Heterosexuals," *Journal of Abnormal Psychology* 82 (1973): 506-13; Marvin Siegelman, "Parental Backgrounds of Homosexual and Heterosexual Men: A Cross National Replication," *Archives of Sexual Behavior* 10 (1981): 505-13.

See additional studies that appear to support the psychoanalytic hypothesis, including Louise B. Apperson and W. George McAdoo Jr., "Parental Factors in the Childhood of Homosexuals," *Journal of Abnormal Psychology* 73 (1968): 201-6; Marcel Saghir and Eli Robins, *Male and Female Homosexuality* (Baltimore: Williams and Wilkins, 1973); John R. Snortum, J. F. Gillespie, J. E. Marshall, J. P. McLaughlin and L. Mosberg, "Family Dynamics and Homosexuality," *Psychological Reports* 24 (1969): 763-70.

[17]Alan P. Bell, Martin S. Weinberg and Sue K. Hammersmith, *Sexual Preference: Its Development in Men and Women* (Bloomington: Indiana University Press, 1981).

theory. However, considerably more homosexual males reported fathers who were detached or not affectionate than did heterosexual men, and 48% of white homosexual males reported negative feelings such as anger, fear or resentment toward their fathers, as compared to 29% of the heterosexual sample. While clearly not providing definitive support for the psychoanalytic hypothesis, this study is surely not the refutation of that hypothesis that it is sometimes supposed to be.

In a review of his work with 200 male homosexuals, Gerard van den Aardweg observed that "79% described their mother as 'overanxious' or 'overconcerned' in relation to them: excessively warning them against dangers of all kinds, preoccupied with their health, oversentimental when their son met with some hardship or misfortune, too anxious about their good manners and good behavior, and the like."[18] Similarly, in 71% of his 200 cases, van den Aardweg observed that "the most important factor [was] the father's detachedness and nonparticipation in the son's upbringing. The fathers of 38% of the men were so hypercritical that the sons were made to feel either rejected and/or inferior."[19] As the report of the work of one clinician, this study is of questionable scientific persuasiveness.

Psychoanalytic theorists posit that certain parenting patterns cause the homosexuality of the child, but it is possible that the causation goes in the other direction. The classic "distant or absent father" and "over-involved mother" can in theory be either the *cause* or *result* of gender nonconformity. For example, cross-sex-typed behavior in a boy of the type discussed earlier (perhaps influenced indirectly by biological variables that are expressed in temperamental differences interacting with environmental circumstances) could contribute to a father's being distant or emotionally unavailable to his son. It is also conceivable that certain experiences (such as the early homosexual experiences we discuss next) may facilitate a same-sex identity adaptation under certain environmental conditions, accelerated perhaps by the contemporary categorization of same-sex identity, that is, to say of oneself, "I am gay."

Childhood sexual experience. Childhood sexual trauma has also been

---

[18]Gerard van den Aardweg, *On the Origins and Treatment of Homosexuality* (New York: Praeger, 1985), p. 183.

[19]Ibid., p. 184.

considered as a factor in the origins of same-sex attraction for some persons. This data has not been generated by any one psychological theory; just about any psychological theory would speculate that early sexual experience would complicate later sexual attraction. Research in support of this connection includes findings from the best national, representative survey on sexual behavior of nearly 3,500 Americans. This study found that among those who had been sexually abused as children, 7.4% of men and 3.1% of women reported a homosexual orientation, whereas among those who were not sexually abused as children, only 2.0% of men and 0.8% of women reported a homosexual orientation.[20] Experience of sexual abuse as a child, in other words, more than tripled the likelihood of later reporting homosexual orientation.

Other studies have reported the same trend. In a much smaller clinical sample, Shrier and Johnson[21] reported that 58% (23 of 40) of adolescent males who reported sexual abuse identified themselves as either homosexual or bisexual. In contrast, of those who did not report a history of sexual abuse, 90% identified themselves as heterosexual.

In a study comparing early sexual behavior among homosexual and heterosexual males, Manosevitz[22] reported that 25% (7 of 28) of male homosexuals reported that between the ages of 5-9 they engaged in childhood sexual activity with other males. In contrast, none of the heterosexual sample reported sexual activity with other males during those years. Between the ages of 10-12, 43% (12 of 28) of male homosexuals reported sexual activity with males, as compared to 9% (2 of 22) of the heterosexual sample.

The findings from these kinds of studies are often overlooked in mainstream publications on gay and lesbian persons. For example, in a recent book[23] published by the American Psychological Association on

---

[20]See table 9.14 in Edward O. Laumann, John H. Gagnon, Robert T. Michael and Stuart Michaels, *The Social Organization of Sexuality: Sexual Practices in the United States* (Chicago: University of Chicago Press, 1994), p. 344.

[21]Diane Shrier and Robert L. Johnson, "Sexual Victimization of Boys: An Ongoing Study of an Adolescent Medicine Clinic Population," *Journal of the National Medical Association* 80 (1988): 1189-93.

[22]Martin Manosevitz, "Early Sexual Behavior in Adult Homosexual and Heterosexual Males," *Journal of Abnormal Psychology* 76 (1970): 396-402.

[23]Bertram J. Cohler, Andrew J. Hostetler and Andrew M. Boxer, "Generativity, Social

generativity and adult development, the authors in the chapter dealing with generativity among gay males discuss three case examples that provide a narrative account of gay men at middle age. It is interesting to note that all three of the gay men reported traumatic experiences early in life and that two of the three reported early sexual debut with members of the same sex. The first man was "only vaguely aware" of attraction to other men before age thirteen, when he had a same-sex experience with a fourteen-year-old male. The same-sex experience reported by the second gay man was actually a gang rape by "several neighborhood boys" when he was only thirteen. The third case study was of a self-identifying gay man who did not report a similar early same-sex sexual debut, but the researchers note that "he had a 'sense' that he was a sissy as a child, and he was singled out for ridicule by his peers."[24] They report he had early experiences of humiliation and trauma, including the loss of his mother to brain cancer when he was twelve years old.

Of course, these experiences and the percentages of childhood sexual abuse noted above make it clear that childhood sexual trauma or sexual activity in childhood or early sexual debut does not directly "cause" homosexuality or experiences of same-sex attraction. If they did, then all, not just some, of the individuals who went through such experiences would turn out homosexual. Same-sex childhood experience may leave a child who also has a secure identification with the same-sex parent basically unaffected. Perhaps adult same-sex attraction is more frequent among those who have experienced childhood sexual trauma or engaged in sexual activity, but this research does not support the idea of a one-to-one correlation. It may also be the case that childhood sexual trauma and sexual activity in childhood may increase the likelihood of adult homosexual feelings by reinforcing same-sex feelings that were already present. From this perspective, studies of gender nonconformity may support psychological/environmental theories for same-sex attraction, but they may also support biological theories.

Context, and Lived Experience: Narratives of Gay Men in Middle Adulthood," in *Generativity and Adult Development: How and Why We Care for the Next Generation*, ed. Dan P. McAdams and Ed de St. Aubin (Washington, D.C.: American Psychological Association), pp. 265-309.

[24]Ibid., p. 286.

Exotic Becomes Erotic theory. Daryl Bem, professor of psychology at Cornell University in New York, has developed a theory[25] for the origins of same-sex attraction that is based on research similar to the studies cited above. He focuses on environmental influences in contrast to biological influences. His theory is the Exotic Becomes Erotic (EBE) theory of sexual orientation, where he proposes that "individuals can become erotically attracted to classes of individuals from whom they felt different during childhood."[26] According to Bem gender polarization is the most common explanation for heterosexuality: "Most cultures, including our own, polarize the sexes, setting up a sex-based division of labor and power, emphasizing or exaggerating sex differences, and, in general, superimposing the male-female dichotomy on virtually every aspect of communal life."[27] Bem suggests that being raised to be most familiar with your same-sex group results in a certain mysteriousness or "exoticness" of the other sex, and what is exotic tends to be regarded as sexually attractive or "erotic" in adult life. The result is that most boys and girls grow up to be sexually attracted to one another. Children who grow up feeling different from their same-sex peers *for gender-related reasons* (i.e., for whom it is members of the same sex who are "exotic") can develop same-sex attraction, which is often (but not always) preceded by a lack of interest in gender-typical toys and activities.

Although Bem is apparently not conducting new research to support his theory, he does cite studies in the existing literature that he believes support his theory. These include the research by Bell, Weinberg and Hammersmith mentioned above, who surveyed a large, nonrepresentative sample of homosexuals in the San Francisco area. Bem reports that

---

[25]Daryl J. Bem, "Exotic Becomes Erotic: A Developmental Theory of Sexual Orientation," *Psychological Review* 103 (1996): 320-35.

[26]Daryl J. Bem, "Is EBE Theory Supported by the Evidence? Is It Androcentric? A Reply to Peplau et al.," *Psychological Review* 105, no. 2 (1998): 395.

[27]Ibid., p. 395. Letitia Peplau and her colleagues at the University of California, Los Angeles, offer a strong critique of Bem's EBE theory. They argue that the research does not support his theory and that the theory itself fails to predict lesbian experiences of sexual identity formation (and so it is decried as "androcentric"). Bem offers a reply in which he argues that Peplau and her colleagues failed to understand his theory and misrepresented the relevance of the existing research to the major tenets of EBE and that the different and more fluid developmental course for lesbians is actually predicted by EBE. See "A Critique of Bem's 'Exotic Becomes Erotic' Theory of Sexual Orientation," *Psychological Reports* 105, no. 2 (1998): 387-94.

"71% of gay men and 70% of lesbians in the San Francisco study reported feeling different from their same-sex peers during childhood, compared with 38% and 51% of heterosexual men and women, respectively."[28] Bem's argument is not that gay men and lesbians felt "different," but that they felt "sexually different" from members of their same-sex during childhood. The gender-based experience of "feeling different" is what Bem argues is central to his theory.

Another piece of "evidence" that Bem cites as support for this theory is the apparent fluidity of female homosexuality as compared to male homosexuality. Bem references the Bell study and the Laumann study as showing that women more often report bisexuality rather than exclusive lesbian identity, whereas men are the opposite. According to Bem his theory anticipates these differences because girls engage in both gender-stereotypical and gender-nonstereotypical activities more often than boys and are more likely to have friends of both sexes: "This implies that girls are less likely than boys to feel differentially different from opposite-sex and same-sex peers and, hence, are less likely to develop exclusively heteroerotic or homoerotic orientations."[29]

Biological Theories

Despite the evidence that supports the various psychological or environmental theories of homosexuality, the past decade has witnessed a dramatic swing toward the biological theories for the origins of sexual orientation. Many assume and explicitly state that the relative lack of attention being paid today to psychological theories should be understood as indicating that these theories have been disproven. The psychological theories have not been refuted; rather, they appear to have been neglected in favor of what many have thought would be more promising research on biological factors. The shift to biology was embraced, at least early on, by proponents of change from the traditional Christian sexual ethic. What made the turn to biology attractive, in part, was its implied refutation of the caricature of traditionalists, who are said to believe homosexual orientation is merely a choice.

The major proposed causes for a biological basis to homosexuality

---

[28]Bem, "Is EBE Theory," p. 396.
[29]Ibid., p. 398.

include the adult hormonal hypothesis, the prenatal hormonal hypothesis and the genetic hypothesis. We will discuss these hypotheses and the current scientific evidence for each, starting with the only hypothesis that is relatively easy to dismiss.

Adult hormonal hypothesis. There is a long tradition of investigating whether male and female homosexuals have abnormal levels of certain sex hormones as compared to their heterosexual peers. Speculation began in the nineteenth century that male homosexuals might lack normal male hormone levels and/or have female hormones and female homosexuals the reverse. Several decades ago reports of findings that seemed to confirm such theories were not uncommon, though never well established.

The consensus today from research on males is that there are no substantial hormonal differences between homosexuals and heterosexuals. Research that was once thought to show hormonal differences in males has been shown to be plagued by problems in measuring hormones and inaccurate ways of categorizing the sexual preferences of those being studied.[30] The results of some studies of lesbians suggest that while most lesbians fall within the normal ranges of adult hormones (serum testosterone and estrogen), a subpopulation of lesbians actually may have elevated testosterone levels. These findings, however, may be more the result of sample selection, stress, occupational affiliation or physical exercise patterns in the samples studied than of lesbianism in itself.[31] In any case, the general consensus among researchers and theorists today is that hormone levels in adulthood do not determine whether a person is homosexual or heterosexual.[32]

Prenatal hormonal hypothesis. Some researchers propose that human sexual orientation is determined before birth, probably between the second and fifth month of pregnancy. It is during this time that the fetus is exposed to sex hormones, its sexual anatomy develops, and its brain is "wired" in a manner appropriate to its biological gender. Could the devel-

---

[30]L. J. G. Gooren, "An Appraisal of Endocrine Theories of Homosexuality and Gender Dysphoria," in *The Pharmacology and Endocrinology of Sexual Function*, Handbook of Sexology, ed. J. M. A. Sitsen (New York: Elsevier, 1988), 6:410-24.

[31]Brian A. Gladue, "Hormones in Relationship to Homosexual/Bisexual/Heterosexual Gender Orientation," in *The Pharmacology and Endocrinology of Sexual Function*, Handbook of Sexology, ed. J. M. A. Sitsen (New York: Elsevier, 1988), 6:388-409.

[32]Ibid., p. 393. For example, Gladue concludes that "it is unlikely that sex hormone levels have any direct bearing on sexual orientation in adults."

opment of homosexuality have its roots in this period of life?

We should stress that hypothesized genetic and prenatal hormonal influences may be independent and exclusive of each other, or they may be interdependent and complementary. It is likely, indeed, that if there is a genetic element to the development of homosexuality, it probably works through prenatal and early childhood hormones.

We should begin our discussion of nature with some cautionary comments about research with animals and how it relates to human sexual orientation. Several studies have looked at manipulations of sex hormone levels in animal fetuses (where researchers inject animal fetuses with abnormally high levels of a sex hormone) to study the effects this has on sexual differentiation and later sexual behavior in adult animals. It has been shown that the abnormal doses of sex hormones injected in an animal prenatally can result in that adult animal showing inverted ("homosexual") behavior when mating.

Some take these findings as evidence that similar hormone variations may be causal factors in human homosexuality.[33] Others argue that there are monumental problems in establishing the relevance of this animal research for human beings. First, highly abnormal hormone levels are needed to create these behaviors, and such high levels seem unlikely in normal human pregnancies.

Second, the fact that experimenters can cause these outcomes by creating highly abnormal conditions by no means leads to the conclusion that "naturally occurring" instances of homosexuality came about because of the same sorts of abnormal conditions. For instance, the fact that delirium can be brought on by striking another's head with a baseball bat hardly implies that the standard cause of most cases of delirium is being hit on the head with a baseball bat.

Third, there are vast differences between animal and human sexual behavior; the sexual behavior of humans is much more complex than the sexual behavior of rats.[34] The normal sexual behavior of rats, for exam-

[33]For example, Lee Ellis and Ashley Ames, "Neurohormonal Functioning and Sexual Orientation: A Theory of Homosexuality-Heterosexuality," *Psychological Bulletin* 101 (1987): 233-38.

[34]Elizabeth Adkins-Regan, "Sex Hormones and Sexual Orientation in Animals," *Psychobiology* 16 (1988): 335-47; William Byne and Bruce Parsons, "Human Sexual Orientation," *Archives of General Psychiatry* 50 (1993): 228-39; H. Feder, "Hormones and Sexual Be-

ple, is more reflexive—an involuntary response to stimulation—than is human behavior. When a female rat is in estrus ("heat"), she will raise reflexively her rump (lordosis) when a male is near to facilitate intercourse. Male rats, when they smell a female in estrus, engage in mounting behavior (just like dogs). In the animals that have been exposed to abnormal hormones, what gets called "homosexual behavior" in rats— such as lordosis in males or mounting by females—occurs as a reflex to sexual stimulation alone *regardless of who or what provides the stimulation.* Such behavior does not indicate what we recognize as an orientation in humans. For example, the male rat exposed to prenatal feminizing hormones will exhibit lordosis in response to the experimenter's hand as easily as to another, normal male rat. Such behavior is a reflex, not the result of an orientation.

We will report on five major types of evidence that are commonly cited to support the prenatal hormone hypothesis. These are (1) the study of the LH feedback cycle, (2) results from pharmacological "quasi experiments" on prenatal hormonal levels, (3) gender nonconformity in childhood, (4) maternal stress during pregnancy and (5) anatomical studies of brain structures of homosexual persons. Some theorists argue on the basis of these types of evidence that homosexuality is biologically determined by prenatal hormones, while others disagree.

1. The LH feedback cycle. In very simple terms, it is well established that mature female rats, when injected with a dose of estrogen, respond soon thereafter with a release in their bodies of luteinizing hormone (LH). Male rats, injected with estrogen, do not demonstrate any such LH surge in response to the estrogen. Researchers speculated that this LH feedback cycle is evidence of a "feminized" brain, the result of the early patterning of the brain that occurs before birth. It has been hypothesized that the LH feedback cycle for male homosexuals would show a positive LH feedback cycle similar to heterosexual females. This hypothesis grew out of the supposition that male homosexuals have feminized or feminine brains. Several early studies reported that male homosexuals did indeed show an LH surge indicative of brain feminization. Subsequent (and

havior," *Annual Review of Psychology* 35 (1984): 165-200; Wendell Ricketts, "Biological Research on Homosexuality: Ansell's Cow or Occam's Razor?" *Journal of Homosexuality* 9 (1984): 65-93.

more sophisticated) research in this area has not clearly or consistently documented findings that supported this hypothesis. It is now generally doubted that the LH response really occurs in human females at all, and the findings about gay men have fallen into some disrepute.[35]

2. *Pharmacological "quasi experiments" on prenatal hormone levels.* It would be unethical to perform experiments that directly manipulated hormones in the womb with human fetuses. However, a number of naturally or accidentally occurring medical conditions have been discussed as quasi experiments of sorts. To illustrate how important such quasi experiments can be in other areas of inquiry, note that a lot of what we know about brain function today derives from such quasi experiments: we cannot destroy sections of the brains of humans to see what that section did (by noting what the injured person can no longer do), but we *can* carefully study people who have sustained accidental brain injury and note what behavioral or cognitive changes go along with destruction of those areas of the brain.

Numerous studies (or quasi experiments) have tracked the children born to mothers who took drugs during pregnancy that were later shown to produce abnormal hormonal environments for their babies in the womb, or who had medical conditions that produced the same effect. The studies of these unfortunate occurrences have shown that some human fetuses exposed to abnormal hormone levels during development can show altered physical development, brain functioning, gender orientation and sexual behavior when mature. For example, one recent study reported that the female children of mothers who unwittingly exposed their fetuses to elevated levels of estrogen by taking a synthetic estrogen drug during pregnancy were (modestly) more likely to become bisexuals (or, much less likely, to become lesbians) as adults.[36]

The relevance of these findings is questionable. First, the homosexual population shows no elevated rates of what we might expect to see of physical abnormalities that often coincide with prenatal hormonal aberrations. Second, the fact that certain outcomes can occur due to

---

[35]See the summary in Byne and Parsons, "Human Sexual Orientation."
[36]Heino F. L. Meyer-Bahlburg, Anke A. Ehrhardt, Laura R. Rosen, Rhoda S. Gruuen, Norma P. Veridiano, Felix H. Vann and Herbert F. Neuwalder, "Prenatal Estrogens and the Development of Homosexual Orientation," *Developmental Psychology* 31 (1995): 12-21.

abnormal conditions (taking a synthetic hormone) by no means leads to the conclusion that "naturally occurring" instances of homosexuality occurred because of the same abnormal conditions; by analogy, the fact that a young child can sustain spinal injuries in a car accident tells us nothing about the spinal abnormalities of a baby with spina bifida. Finally, few of the unfortunate subjects in these "quasi experiments" develop a clear or "pure" homosexual identity apart from other broad disruptions of gender identity and behavior. In other words, the children studied in these quasi experiments often have many deep and varied problems in a way that dwarfs those of the typical homosexual person. This fact makes comparison with the homosexual population problematic.

3. *Gender nonconformity in childhood.* Another type of evidence cited in support of prenatal causation of homosexuality in humans includes those studies mentioned above on gender nonconformity or gender inappropriateness early in childhood. Boys who are strikingly effeminate as young children appear to be much more likely to become homosexual men than their more typically masculine peers; the reverse holds true for highly masculinized females. Researchers who promote the prenatal hormone hypothesis argue that such early abnormal patterns must be based in a biological process at work since conception.

While the argument may be correct, this is weak supporting evidence for two reasons. First, some gender-atypical children do not grow up to be homosexual, and some homosexuals do not report gender nonconformity as children. Second, and more importantly, there is no conclusive understanding of why early nonconformity occurs. The fact that the behavior patterns are noticed early (usually in the second or third years of life) does not make them biological in origin. Although some regard these patterns as evidence for the prenatal hormonal hypothesis, others, as we mentioned above, view these studies as evidence that the causes are psychological or environmental. Proponents of psychological causation, as we noted earlier, can claim that the powerful forces of the family are at work at an early age. Proponents of the role of early sexual experiences might also argue that gender atypicality may less mean that the young child is a "prehomosexual" and more that the child is likely to be more vulnerable to being targeted for sexual advances in childhood.

4. *Maternal stress during pregnancy.* An additional area of study has been

maternal stress during pregnancy, which some researchers propose as a predisposing influence on the development of homosexuality. The most frequently cited studies in support of this hypothesis are those by Dorner showing that an unusual number of homosexuals were born to German women who were pregnant during World War II. Dorner developed the hypothesis that the male babies these women were carrying were exposed to unusual hormonal fluctuations in their mother's womb that were the result of the mothers being exposed to such horrific (and physiologically stressful) conditions as bombings and nearby combat.[37] These hypothesized conditions resulted, in Dorner's mind, in the noted elevated rates of male homosexuality in postwar Germany. This indirect evidence for a prenatal hypothesis could also be seen as supporting other psychological theories of causation. Note, for instance, that these same young German boys were often raised without fathers (given how many German men were killed in World War II); this presents a substantial challenge to male identity formation.

Some also point to studies of birth order (homosexual men being born later in the birth order) and studies that show homosexual men as more likely to have more brothers compared to sisters (in one recent study[38] the ratio was approximately 1.5 to 1). Some theorists argue that the mothers of homosexuals are more likely to have been stressed, which tends to result in more male births and is hypothesized to create androgen insufficiency, which would lead to incomplete masculinization of the male fetus (and result in homosexuality in adulthood).

5. Anatomical brain structures. The last major area of evidence cited to support the prenatal hormonal theory for homosexuality has to do with differences in certain specific anatomical structures of the brain. Researchers who favor the prenatal hypothesis study structures in the brain that depend on certain hormones and may be related to atypical gender role behavior among some homosexuals.

The three key areas that have receive a tremendous amount of media attention include

---

[37]See the summaries in Ellis and Ames, "Neurohormonal Functioning," or in Byne and Parsons, "Human Sexual Orientation."

[38]Ray Blanchard, Kenneth J. Zucker, Susan J. Bradley and Caitlin S. Hume, "Birth Order and Sibling Sex Ratio in Homosexual Male Adolescents and Probably Prehomosexual Feminine Boys," *Developmental Psychology* 31 (1995): 22-30.

☐ An area of the hypothalamus referred to as the suprachiasmic nucleus (SCN). Swaab and Hofman,[39] researchers at the Institute for Brain Research at Amsterdam University, have reported that this area was larger among heterosexual males than homosexual males.

☐ An area of the corpus callosum (referred to as the midsagittal plane of the anterior commissure, or MPAC), the narrow structure of the brain that connects the right and left hemispheres. Allen and Gorski,[40] researchers at the UCLA School of Medicine, reported that this structure was about the same size on average among heterosexual females and homosexual males but was larger in both of these groups than among heterosexual males.

☐ Another area of the hypothalamus (the portion of the hypothalamus referred to as the interstitial nucleus of the anterior hypothalamus 3, or INAH3). Simon LeVay,[41] a neurobiologist who performed his research at the Salk Institute in California, reported that this area was larger among heterosexual males than homosexual males and heterosexual females.

The tremendous attention paid to these studies in the media has obscured some of the problems they present. To understand the complexity of this area of research, we have assembled the findings of all of the major studies of these areas and others to date in table 3.1. Let us discuss three major problems with this research in light of all the findings.

First, careful study of this table will reveal that a number of these studies conflict with other studies or have not been replicated (that is, the identical results have not been repeated in other laboratories). Note that the results reported on brain regions INAH1, INAH2 and the MPAC have conflicted, with other studies reporting no differences or differences that point in the opposite direction.

Second, there are problems in interpreting these differences. The finding of Swaab and Hofman of an SCN difference has not yet been repli-

---

[39]Dick F. Swaab and Michael A. Hofman, "An Enlarged Suprachiasmic Nucleus in Homosexual Men," *Brain Research* 537 (1990): 141-48.

[40]Laura Allen and Roger A. Gorski, "Sexual Orientation and the Size of the Anterior Commissure in the Human Brain," *Proceedings of the National Academy of Science USA* 89 (1992): 7199-202.

[41]Simon LeVay, "A Difference in the Hypothalamic Structure Between Heterosexual and Homosexual Men," *Science* 253 (1991): 1034-37.

Study	Brain Region						
	INAH1	INAH2	INAH3	INAH4	SCN	SDNH	MPAC
Swaab & Fliers (1985)	HetM > HetF						
Allen et al. (1989)	HetM = HetF	HetM > HetF	HetM > HetF	HetM = HetF			
LeVay (1991)	HetM = Het F	HetM = HetF	HetM > (HetF & HomM)	HetM = HetF			
Swaab & Hofman (1988)						HetM = Hom M; (HetM & HomM) > Het F	
Swaab & Hofman (1990)					HomM > HetM; shape spherical in HetM; elongated in HomM and HetF		

Allen & Gorski (1991)					HetF > HetM
Allen & Gorski (1992)					(HetF = HomM) > HetM
Demeter et al. (1988)					HetF < HetM

Table 3.1. Brain differences between heterosexual and homosexual men and heterosexual women. The references for each study cited are: Dick F. Swaab and E. Fliers, "A Sexually Dimorphic Nucleus in the Human Brain," *Science* 228 (1985): 1112-14; Simon LeVay, "A Difference in the Hypothalamic Structure Between Heterosexual and Homosexual Men," *Science* 253 (1991): 1034-37; Laura Allen, M. Hines, J. E. Shryne and Roger A Gorski, "Two Sexually Dimorphic Cell Groups in the Human Brain," *Journal of Neuroscience* 9 (1989): 497-506; Dick F. Swaab and Michael Hofman, "Sexual Differentiation of the Human Hypothalamus: Ontogeny of the Sexually Dimorphic Nucleus of the Preoptic Area," *Developmental Brain Research* 44 (1988): 314-18; Dick F. Swaab and Michael Hofman, "An Enlarged Suprachiasmic Nucleus in Homosexual Men," *Brain Research* 537 (1990): 141-48; Laura Allen and Roger A. Gorski, "Sexual Dimorphism of the Anterior Commissure and Massa Intermedia of the Human Brain," *Journal of Comparative Neurology* 312 (1991): 97-104; L. Allen and R. A. Gorski, "Sexual Orientation and the Size of the Anterior Commissure in the Human Brain," *Proceedings of the National Academy of Science USA* 89 (1992): 7199-202; S. Demeter, J. L. Ringo and R. W Doty, "Morphometric Analysis of the Human Corpus Callosum and the Anterior Commissure," *Human Neurobiology* 6 (1988): 219-26.

INAH means interstitial nucleus of the anterior hypothalamus (four different sections of the interstitial nucleus of the anterior hypothalamus have been examined and are here designated by the numbers 1-4); SCN means suprachiasmic nucleus, SDNH means sexually dimorphic nucleus of the hypothalamus, and MPAC means midsagittal plane of the anterior commissure. In the body of the table, < symbolizes "was significantly smaller than"; > symbolizes "was significantly larger than"; = symbolizes "no size difference noted"; HetF = Heterosexual Female; HomM = Homosexual Male; HetM = Heterosexual Male. A blank cell means that area of the brain was not examined in the study reported on that row.

cated. But even if it eventually is, its significance is questionable since the SCN does not differ in size according to sex and has no known role in regulating sexual behavior.[42]

Finally, some of the studies suffer from serious methodological flaws. For example, consider the problems in the study conducted by Simon LeVay. First, the LeVay study examined only 35 people (which is a very small number of people for research purposes). Second, questions have been raised about the fashion in which LeVay determined the orientation of the persons whose brains he was dissecting after death. Nineteen of the men were assigned the designation homosexual based on it being noted in their medical charts by their doctors; the remaining 16 men were presumed to be heterosexual *on the basis that their sexual orientation was not mentioned in their charts*. This leads us to suspect that LeVay did not know for sure whether the brains of nearly half of the people he was studying were from homosexual or heterosexual persons. Furthermore, all of the homosexual men and six of the presumed 16 heterosexual men died of AIDS. What is important about this fact is that (1) it makes the supposition that the six "heterosexual" men who died of AIDS were heterosexual seem questionable, and (2) AIDS and the medications used to treat HIV infection can affect the size and shape of the very part of the brain LeVay was studying. We do not know whether his findings are related to homosexuality or to the medications used to treat HIV.[43]

In any case, there is no direct evidence yet that exposure to certain prenatal hormones "causes" homosexuality in even a subset of homosexual persons. There is some indirect evidence, although much of it has yet to be replicated, and for some studies, serious methodological questions remain.

Genetic hypothesis. The genetic theories propose, in some fashion or another, that homosexuality is determined at the moment of conception. Proponents are quite hazy on the manner in which the genes are thought to cause sexual orientation; some seem to imply that they favor direct causation (the possibility of a "gay gene") while others suggest that some

---

[42]Byne and Parsons, "Human Sexual Orientation," p. 235.
[43]For a more extensive critique of LeVay's research and the other studies on neuroanatomical differences, see ibid., pp. 228-39.

sort of indirect causation is more likely (that is, that some characteristics other than sexual orientation combine to make it more likely the child will grow up homosexual).

There are two major types of research in support of the genetic hypothesis. Only recently have researchers been able to look directly at the genetic material, and so we will examine these "direct" genetic studies last. Long before such studies were possible, "indirect" genetic studies examined the ways in which certain characteristics (whether physical or behavioral) seemed to be passed on from parents to children and whether these patterns seemed to follow patterns we understood to indicate genetic causes. The indirect genetic studies look at the likelihood that siblings or other family members will share the characteristic being studied, in this case, homosexuality or experiences of same-sex attraction. The rate at which genetically related persons share similar characteristics is referred to as the *concordance rate.*

1. Indirect genetic studies. The earliest research[44] into genetic factors in homosexuality reported a 100% concordance rate for homosexuality in identical twins—whenever one twin was homosexual, his co-twin was reported to be homosexual *in every instance.* This suggested an utterly deterministic genetic cause (like eye color). But these results did not withstand further tests, and the researcher himself apparently later referred to his results as a "statistical artifact."[45] For a period of time it then became the trend to deny that *any* genetic factors were active in the causation of homosexuality at all, leading secular experts on human sexuality to comment as late as 1992 that "the genetic theory of homosexuality has been generally discarded today."[46]

Nevertheless, interest in genetics as a possible cause of homosexuality began to grow through the 1980s. For example, Richard Green[47] reviewed previously published studies of the frequency of homosexuality

[44]F. J. Kallman, "Comparative Twin Study on the Genetic Aspects of Male Homosexuality," *Journal of Nervous and Mental Disease* 115 (1952): 137-59.

[45]Cited in A. Cooper, "The Aetiology of Homosexuality," in *Understanding Homosexuality,* ed. John A. Loraine (New York: American Elsevier, 1974), pp. 1-24.

[46]William Masters, Virginia Johnson and Robert Kolodny, *Human Sexuality,* 4th ed. (Glenview, Ill.: Scott, Foresman, 1992), p. 390.

[47]Richard Green, "The Immutability of (Homo) Sexual Orientation: Behavioral Science Implications for a Constitutional (Legal) Analysis," *The Journal of Psychiatry and Law* 16 (1988): 537-75.

in identical twins, fraternal twins and near-relatives of homosexuals and argued that homosexuality seemed to cluster in certain families in a manner that suggested genetic underpinnings. He argued that there must be some degree of genetic influence in the origins of homosexuality for some persons. In the last several years there has indeed been much more interest—both in scientific journals and in the popular media—in looking at genetic explanations for homosexuality.

We will focus on the studies that have exerted the greatest influence and that are the most scientifically sophisticated. Michael Bailey, a researcher at Northwestern University, and Richard Pillard, a researcher at Boston University School of Medicine, published separate studies of male[48] and female[49] homosexuality, studies that have received a tremendous amount of attention and have advanced the genetic hypothesis. Before we mention their findings, think for a moment about inheritance of genetically determined characteristics. Identical twins (or monozygotic, from "one egg") share the exact same genes since they are formed from only one egg and one sperm, and hence they always are the same sex and have the same eye color. In fact, they are identical on every biological characteristic that is caused by the genes. Fraternal twins (or dizygotic, from "two eggs") are formed from the mother's releasing more than one egg, with each egg being fertilized by a different sperm. The two fraternal twins are formed from different eggs and different sperm. Fraternal twins, then, can be different sexes and have different genetically determined characteristics such as eye color. Fraternal twins share the same basic degree of genetic similarities as any two siblings born to the same two parents. Finally, adopted siblings will bear no more genetic similarity to the "biological family members" of the adopted family than the general population. So if we are looking at a behavioral pattern we believe to be genetically caused, we will expect identical twins to be the most similar on that variable, then fraternal twins and biological siblings, then half-siblings, and then (and finally) adopted children and the general population.

---

[48] J. Michael Bailey and Richard C. Pillard, "A Genetic Study of Male Sexual Orientation," *Archives of General Psychiatry* 48 (1991): 1081-96.

[49] J. Michael Bailey, Richard C. Pillard, Michael C. Neale and Yvonne Agyei, "Heritable Factors Influence Sexual Orientation in Women," *Archives of General Psychiatry* 50 (1993): 217-23.

In their study of male homosexuals, Bailey and Pillard searched for members of the gay community who were twins and investigated the sexual orientations of their siblings. They reported a "probandwise concordance" of 52%, a statistic widely interpreted by many (including us) as a finding that 52% of the identical twins they located shared their homosexual preference with their brothers. In contrast, they reported a probandwise concordance of only 22% for fraternal twins. The percentages were even lower for other sibling relationships (9.2% for nontwin brothers and 11% for adoptive brothers). Similarly, their study of female homosexuals reported a probandwise concordance of 48%, interpreted most commonly as 48% of the identical twins sharing a homosexual preference. Again, in contrast, they reported only a 16% concordance for fraternal twins, 14% for nontwin sisters and 6% for adoptive sisters. Obviously, this pattern of results parallels what we sketched at the end of the last paragraph as the expected pattern for a characteristic caused by genetic factors: identical twins were most alike on these variables, and other sorts of siblings less so. They concluded that genetics explain a significant amount of the reason why people have a homosexual orientation.

It would be hard to overestimate the broad influence of the Bailey and Pillard studies. They were widely trumpeted in the secular and religious media. To many they are definitive proof that homosexuality is genetic. When a member of the lay public states with confidence "Homosexuality is genetically caused," it is almost always the Bailey and Pillard studies they have vaguely in mind.

We raised several concerns about these studies in our earlier discussions of them,[50] concerns that made these studies less persuasive to us than many others took them to be. The major concern was with the way in which Bailey and Pillard obtained the twins for their studies. Twins involved in the studies were found through advertisements in openly pro-gay magazines and tabloids. It seemed conceivable that since the ads stated that the researchers were looking for gay men and lesbians with twin or same-sex adopted siblings, some people may have been drawn to the study if they believed it would produce benefits for the gay community, the types of benefits that confirmation of the

---

[50]Stanton L. Jones and Mark A. Yarhouse, "Science and the Ecclesiastical Homosexuality Debates," *Christian Scholar's Review* 26, no. 4 (1997): 446-77.

genetic hypothesis would be thought to produce. Homosexuals who had homosexual twins may have been more likely to volunteer than those who did not. This is the problem that researchers call sample bias—if the study method tends to recruit gay twins who have gay co-twins more than those who have twin siblings who are not gay, then the findings may be biased.

The possibility that the Bailey and Pillard studies were plagued by sample bias seemed likely given the failure of other similar studies to produce similar findings with other populations. While one other study to date has published similar findings,[51] other researchers have failed to produce similar results. A smaller study than Bailey and Pillard's studies reported a shared homosexual preference among only 10% of male and female identical twins (if bisexuals are not counted as homosexual) or 25% (if bisexuals are counted).[52] The higher estimate is still half that of the rates for a shared homosexual preference reported by Bailey and Pillard (25% compared to 52%).

Research on identical twins reared apart since birth[53] has also challenged the Bailey and Pillard findings. The researchers who have been studying a small sample of twins reared apart reported that none of the four female identical twin pairs in which one was a homosexual twin shared a homosexual preference. One male twin pair shared a homosexual preference, and one male twin pair did not. The lack of shared homosexual preference for female homosexuals is quite striking when compared to Bailey and Pillard's remarkably high rate of shared homosexual preference for lesbians.

But the decisive refutation of the original findings has come from a recent study by Bailey himself, one that was first reported verbally at a conference[54]

[51] Frederick L. Whitam, Milton Diamond and James Martin, "Homosexual Orientation in Twins: A Report on Sixty-One Pairs and Three Triplet Sets," *Archives of Sexual Behavior* 22 (1993): 187-206.

[52] Michael King and Elizabeth McDonald, "Homosexuals Who Are Twins: A Study of 46 Probands," *British Journal of Psychiatry* 160 (1992): 407-9.

[53] Elke Eckert, Thomas J. Bouchard, Joseph Bohlen and Leonard L. Heston, "Homosexuality in Monozygotic Twins Reared Apart," *British Journal of Psychiatry* 148 (1986): 421-25.

[54] Michael Bailey, "Genetics, Heritability, and Family Influences on Sexual Orientation" (paper presented as part of the symposium "Current Directions in Sex Research," Brian Gladue (chair), Annual Convention of the American Psychological Association, Toronto,

and has only recently moved to published form.[55] Bailey's own reported results would appear to stand as proof that his samples from the earlier studies with Pillard were biased in exactly the manner we hypothesized. Bailey got access to a sample of identical twins that is immune from sample bias: he was allowed to send a survey to all those registered in the Twin Registry of the nation of Australia. By obtaining a sample from all twins born in that country, Bailey eliminated all potential sample biases.

He sent his questionnaire on sexual preferences and experiences to the entire sample and found substantially less concordance (matching) for homosexual orientation between identical and fraternal twins than in the earlier two studies. The influence of genetics on development of homosexual orientation would appear to be, on the basis of this much-improved research, much less than the estimates from the earlier research, as table 3.2 shows.

To understand just how dramatically this new study shrinks the estimation of the influence of genetics on the development of homosexuality, we will have to compare these new results with the older findings in some detail. The reader might glance at this table and note, for instance, that the probandwise concordance for male identical twins has shrunk from 52% to 20%, and regard this as a dramatic decrease in genetic influence. But this fails to tell the whole story.

Bailey's statistical methods as detailed in the new study leave ample room for confusion, though they may have academic merit. The probandwise concordances in the table above are no ordinary percentages. In his new report Bailey is clearer about how this statistic is calculated than he was in the original studies with Pillard. Look at the report

[54]Ontario, Canada, August 12, 1996).

[55]J. Michael Bailey, Michael P. Dunne and Nicholas G. Martin, "Genetic and Environmental Influences on Sexual Orientation and Its Correlates in an Australian Twin Sample," *Journal of Personality and Social Psychology* 78 (March 2000): 33. Bailey is to be commended for his scientific integrity in publishing these findings that stand in such sharp contrast to the results of his earlier studies and for commenting in this manuscript so openly on how these results contradict his earlier conclusions. Christian readers should also take note of the lessons here: first, that science at least partially lives up to its claim of being a self-correcting enterprise, and second, that full understanding of complicated phenomena often requires patience and a willingness to watch for progress in our understandings.

	Bailey & Pillard Males	Bailey Australian Males	Bailey & Pillard Females	Bailey Australian Females
Identical Twins	"29/56" 52% PC	3 of 27 20% PC	"34/71" 48% PC	3 of 22 24% PC
Fraternal Twins	"12/54" 22% PC	0 of 16 0% PC	"6/37" 16% PC	1 of 18 10% PC
Non-Twin Siblings	"13/142" 9% PC	Not reported	"10/73" 14% PC	Not reported
Adopted Siblings	"6/57" 11% PC	Not reported	"2/35" 6% PC	Not reported

Table 3.2. A comparison of probandwise concordance rates across twin studies. "X of Y" should be read as "X pairs of twins were concordant for homosexuality (i.e., both homosexual) out of a total of Y twin pairs." "PC" means probandwise concordance.

of 20% probandwise concordance for male identical twins. Any reader can notice that 3 pairs concordant out of 27 is not 20%; rather, 11% of the pairs (3 divided by a total of 27) were concordant for homosexuality. The 20% statistic comes from counting every concor: dant pair *twice* (in both the numerator and the denominator: 3+3 or 6 divided by 27+3 or 30) with the justification that Bailey is counting "matches," and so for each member of a homosexual twin pair, each member of the pair is a match with the other, for two matches per pair.

This clarifies that even in the earlier research, the report of 52% probandwise concordance for identical twin males *did not mean* that half of all identical twin pairs where one member was gay would find the other twin gay as well. Instead of 29 twin pairs out of 56 total sharing the trait of homosexuality, the apparent meaning of "29/56" is that there were 13 twin pairs concordant for homosexuality, one triplet trio that was concordant, and 27 twin pairs that were *not* concordant for homosexuality. So there were a total of (13+1+27 =) 41 pairs, of which both were homosexual in 14 pairs. Fourteen divided by 41 equals 34%; so 34% of the pairs were concordant for homosexuality in the original study by the common understanding of "concordant," and even that turns out to be an inflated estimate by a factor of three. The original studies *actually* suggested that about a third of male identical twin pairs were concordant, but the new, superior study suggests that the actual concordance rate (as that term is commonly used) for male identical twin pairs is only about 11%.

Given the unprecedented impact of the earlier Bailey and Pillard studies on the public understanding of causation of homosexuality, we cannot resist underscoring what these new findings mean.

First, they mean that *the samples of those earlier studies were biased, dramatically biased.* Bailey and his colleagues were quite clear on this in drawing their conclusions from their new findings: "This suggests that concordances from prior studies [i.e., his own two prior studies] were inflated due to concordance dependent ascertainment bias"[56] (or, in other words, sample bias).

Second, these new findings *call into question whether or not there is a significant genetic influence involved in the causation of homosexuality.* Again,

---

[56] Ibid., p. 534.

Bailey and his coauthors are commendably precise about the implications of their new research, commenting that this study "did not provide statistically significant support for the importance of genetic factors" for homosexual orientation.[57] Genetics may not be important after all in causing homosexuality![58]

We feel it worth noting that there were other problems with the results of the original Bailey and Pillard studies. If genetics was a key to shared homosexual preference, then there should have been very little difference in rates of shared homosexual preference between fraternal twins and nontwin siblings because, as we mentioned earlier, fraternal twins and regular siblings share the same degree of genetic relatedness. However, Bailey and Pillard found the fraternal twin brothers to have twice the rate of shared homosexual preference as nontwin brothers (the female fraternal twins and nontwins siblings reported a similar rate of

---

[57]Ibid., p. 534.

[58]In his verbal conference report Bailey minimized contrast between his earlier studies and the Australian findings. In making this argument he actually reported two different versions of the Australian findings (in the published version he again reported his results in two different versions but did not make the following argument as forcefully). To understand the differences, the reader must understand the ambiguities of how researchers define "homosexual." Bailey went back to Kinsey's famous 7-point graduated scale of sexual orientation from 0 (exclusively heterosexual), 1 (heterosexual with some incidental homosexual behavior or attraction during the lifetime) and so forth through 6 (exclusively homosexual). Bailey reported that the Australian sample had reported themselves to be 82% Kinsey "0s" (exclusively heterosexual). The most common non-zero score was 1 (heterosexual with some incidental homosexual behavior or attraction during the lifetime). The crucial question for the definition of homosexuality is "Where on the scale from 0 to 6 do you begin to define the population as homosexual?" Are the people who rate themselves as 6s homosexual? Or 5s and 6s? Or 4s, 5s and 6s? The statistics we reported in this paragraph in the body of this chapter were the ones that came from defining any score greater than a 1 (i.e., a 2 or above) as homosexual. This seems like a fairly broad definition of homosexuality. Surprisingly to us, however, Bailey argued in his verbal presentation that those endorsing a 1 (heterosexual with some incidental homosexual behavior or attraction during the lifetime) were best understood as "partly gay." Based on this questionable logic (which basically claims that anyone who has ever had *any* homosexual thought, attraction or experience, even of the most incidental sort, is "partly gay" and should be classified with exclusive homosexuals), Bailey reported a second version of his findings using this "more inclusive" (and, to us, utterly invalid) categorization. Those findings were of 37.5% probandwise concordance for identical male twins (9/39); 30% probandwise concordance for identical female twins (14/79); 6.3% probandwise concordance for fraternal male twins (1/31); and 30% probandwise concordance for fraternal female twins (8/45).

concordance). It is also worth noting that the adopted children in these families reported much higher than expected homosexuality rates, a finding that Bailey did not acknowledge. If we estimate the rate of male homosexuality at 3% and female homosexuality at 2%, then these general rates compare strikingly with the 11% and 6% rates reported by Bailey for adopted siblings. There would appear to be some influence at work in these families that raised the homosexuality rates more than threefold; this increase cannot be accounted for by genetics.[59]

The original Bailey and Pillard studies made a huge splash in the popular media; only time will tell if Bailey's follow-up Australian study is ever brought to the public's awareness with the same forcefulness.[60]

Direct genetic studies. In addition to twin studies, the genetic hypothesis has received some support from research on chromosomal markers that may be associated with a homosexual preference. A study by Dean Hamer and his colleagues[61] published in 1993 was heralded as finding the "gay gene." The researchers began with a hypothesis that there are different types of homosexuality and that one of those types may be passed on genetically through the mother's genes (in particular, the X gene that participates in determining sex). They recruited a group of 76 men out of an AIDS treatment program, all of whom reported a strong pattern of homosexual orientation in *maternal* relatives but not in paternal relatives *and* who had a homosexual brother. Looking only at this select group, the researchers examined the X chromosomes in those men in the study. Among the 40 pairs of homosexual brothers in the study, 33 pairs shared a concordance for a certain region of the sex chromosome.

---

[59]One other technical problem with these studies is worth mention in a footnote. The statistical estimates of genetic influence ("heritability") produced by Bailey and his colleagues have to be regarded as speculative, as they had to incorporate into their statistical models estimates of the amount of error in the population and estimates of the base rate of homosexuality in the general population. The error estimates they used were, frankly, a blind guess, but incredibly, they used the widely discarded estimate of 10% for their population base rate estimate for homosexuality, a grossly overinflated estimate.

[60]Stanton L. Jones and Mark A. Yarhouse, "The Incredibly Shrinking Gay Gene," *Christianity Today*, October 4, 1999, p. 53.

[61]Dean H. Hamer, Stella Hu, Victoria L. Magnuson, Nan Hu and A. M. L. Pattatucci, "A Linkage Between DNA Markers on the X Chromosome and Male Sexual Orientation," *Science* 261 (1993): 320-26. In their study 33 of 40 pairs of homosexual brothers shared a significant concordance for the Xq28 subtelomeric region of the sex chromosome.

This was far above the expected random concurrence level of 20 pairs or 50%, leading the researchers to postulate that this chromosomal region may be involved in determining sexual orientation.

A second study[62] by the same research team replicated the findings and extended the investigation. Three important findings came from this research. First, this study produced nearly identical results on the original findings about gay brothers with a new sample of homosexual males. Twenty-two of 32 brothers shared the same chromosomal markers. Second, the original study only looked at genetic material shared by gay male brothers and did not check to make sure that that material was not shared by the research subjects' nongay brothers. If nongay brothers shared the same genetic makeup as well, then the chromosomal region may have been related to a shared family trait rather than sexual orientation. The second study found that nongay brothers were less likely to share this same marker, and this finding increases the likelihood that the marker is related in some way to sexual orientation. A third difference in this study is that the researchers also reported on a sample of lesbian sisters. No significant relationship was found between lesbian sisters and this same chromosomal marker, which suggests that this region is unrelated to female homosexuality.

There are, naturally, problems and limitations with the Hamer studies as well. First, we would again mention replication. A recent attempt by a Canadian laboratory to replicate Hamer's findings failed.[63] The researchers had a larger sample (52 gay sibling pairs) but found no significant relationship of homosexual orientation to this genetic region despite examining four separate chromosomal markers.[64] Similar findings in the

---

[62]Stella Hu, Angela M. L. Pattatucci, Chavis Patterson, Lin Li, David W. Fulker, Stacey S. Cherny, Leonid Kruglyak and Dean H. Hamer, "Linkage Between Sexual Orientation and Chromosome Xq28 in Males but Not in Females." *Nature Genetics* 11 (1995): 248-56.
[63]Georgy Rice, Carol Anderson, Neil Risch and George Ebers, "Male Homosexuality: Absence of Linkage to Microsatellite Markers at Xq28," *Science* 284 (April 1999): 665-67.
[64]Ibid., p. 666. The four chromosomal markers studied were DXS1113, BGN, Factor 8 and DXS1108. Each of these is located on the Xq28 region of the X chromosome. The researchers state: "It is unclear why our results are so discrepant from Hamer's original study. Because our study was larger than that of Hamer et al., we certainly had adequate power to detect a genetic effect as large as was reported in that study. Nonetheless, our data do not support the presence of a gene of large effect influencing sexual orientation at position Xq28" (p. 667).

last decade of "genes for" manic depression, violence, alcoholism and schizophrenia have often failed replication or have been formally retracted. The Hamer et al. results may not stand up over time.

Our major concern with these Hamer et al. studies has to do with their limitations rather than with any particular scientific failing per se. When this research was published, writers of popular news magazine articles asked, "Is There a 'Gay Gene'?"[65] But the question itself is misleading (unless the answer is clear to the public: "No"). The public understanding of this research is that the answer to the headline question, "Is there a gay gene?" is yes. The public usually fails to understand that these researchers may have identified certain chromosomal markers that may play a part in contributing to same-sex attraction for a subgroup of those who experience same-sex attraction. In other words, for a subgroup, a subpopulation, of persons who experience homosexual attraction, these markers may play a role in experiences of same-sex attraction.

We are making two points here. First, Hamer and his colleagues did not find a "gay gene" because they did not look at "gays" in general. Rather, they only found this marker among male homosexuals, and in particular, only among those who showed strong "maternal transmission" in their family trees and who had a gay brother. Whether male homosexuals who manifest such maternal transmission are a large or small portion of gays is unclear. Certainly, pairs of homosexual brothers are not that common. Second, and of equal importance, the researchers found that this chromosomal pattern was neither necessary nor sufficient to cause homosexuality. If it was necessary to the homosexual condition, then they would not have found the 7 out of 40 homosexual brother pairs who did not share this characteristic (these 7 brothers did not have the chromosomal pattern but were gay anyway). If it was sufficient to cause homosexuality, then they would not have found, in their second study, nonhomosexual brothers who shared the genetic characteristic but not the sexual orientation (these brothers did have the marker but were not gay). Having the genetic marker does not mean you are a homosexual (not sufficient), and not having the genetic marker does not mean that you are not a homosexual (not necessary). If the Hamer findings stand,

[65]Traci Watson, Joseph P. Shapiro, Jim Impoco and Timothy M. Ito, "Is There a 'Gay Gene'?" *U.S. News & World Report*, November 13, 1995, p. 93.

they provide us with interesting evidence of something important, but of what remains to be seen.

These findings may point to chromosomal patterns that do not cause sexual orientation as such but rather that cause certain temperamental or other variables that make same-sex attraction more likely to occur among a subset of persons who experience homosexual attraction. The causal relationship between these markers and homosexuality may be indirect rather than direct.

Interestingly, a research team including Dean Hamer recently published a study[66] on whether there is a genetic link to cigarette smoking behavior. Their results suggest that there may be a relationship between specific genes and the ability to quit smoking. Their research produced support for the following hypotheses: some people appear to have a genetic predisposition toward novelty-seeking behavior, a need for more stimulation and excitement. People without the identified gene were more likely to smoke and keep smoking. In an interview Dean Hamer stated that the identified gene

> is not a strict determinant of the ability to quit smoking, but rather an influence on an individual's general need and responsiveness to external stimuli, of which cigarette smoking is but one example.[67]

The identified gene alters a particular version of a chemical transporter process in the brain, which may reduce the need for novelty and stimulation. One type of novelty and stimulation these people can do without more easily than those without the gene is cigarettes. A similar statement might help clarify the state of scientific knowledge about homosexuality. Rather than comparing same-sex attraction to race or eye color, both of which are completely determined by our genes, the more accurate parallel with regard to genetic causation, may be to cigarette smoking. The chromosomal markers mentioned above may signal personality or temperamental traits that make experiences of same-sex attraction more or less

---

[66]Sue Z. Sabol, Mark L. Nelson, Lorraine Gunzerath, Cindy L. Brody, Stella Hu, Leo A. Sirota, Stephen E. Marcus, Benjamin D. Greenberg, Frank R. Lucas IV, Jonathon Benjamin, Dennis L. Murphy and Dean H. Hamer, "A Genetic Association for Cigarette Smoking Behavior," *Health Psychology* 18, no. 1 (1999): 7-13.

[67]Pam Willenz, "APA News Release" (APA Public Affairs Office, January 14, 1999), available at <www.apa.org/releases/smoke99.html>.

interesting to an individual under certain circumstances. It is possible that some people have genetically grounded personality traits that predispose the person toward, but do not "cause," homosexuality. Perhaps they have the types of temperaments that make it more difficult to fully identify as a typical man or woman. Perhaps they crave the forbidden or exotic. Perhaps they experience sexual arousal to a wider array of stimuli. Perhaps they have the physical appearance that makes them attractive to same-sex partners. If they have additional experiences that promote same-sex interests and sexual identification (including cultural or subcultural support), they may very well identify or experience themselves as gay or lesbian.[68]

Conclusion on Causality

The genetic hypothesis and the prenatal hormonal hypothesis (especially as supposedly manifested in brain structure) are "hot" right now. Although there is an impressive amount of research cited in favor of these hypotheses, the direct research in support of each of them is inconclusive at this time. Bailey's recent study, in fact, casts significant doubt on the significance of genetics in the causation of homosexuality. On the other hand, there is a substantial amount of research on psychological/ environmental factors that is being generally ignored today despite the findings represented in the literature. It is worth remembering that the recent movement toward biological theories may be as much due to political forces as any real or empirical or scientific dissatisfaction with the psychosocial theories.

In any case, researchers William Byne and Bruce Parsons effectively communicate the caution we must have when looking for the "cause" of homosexuality:

---

[68]In this sense, identifying oneself as gay or lesbian may be traced to a combination of both essentialist and social constructionist claims. On the one hand, there may be some genetic markers that could be viewed as supporting an essentialist perspective that sexual orientation is a real thing or essence (although the possible existence of such markers does not logically support expansive forms of essentialism where behaviors that express that essence are deemed moral in and of themselves). At the same time, those genetic markers may really signal personality or temperamental differences that make same-sex attraction more compelling. Under certain circumstances (e.g., childhood sexual trauma, disordered parent-child relationships, etc.) and in a social context that supports same-sex self-identification, some people may identify themselves as gay or lesbian. The combination of variables undoubtedly varies from person to person and across cultures.

Recent studies postulate biological factors as the primary basis for sexual orientation. However, there is no evidence at present to substantiate a biological theory, just as there is no compelling evidence to support any singular psychosocial explanation.[69]

For those who are trying to gather information from science on the origins of homosexuality, we would conclude that no research to date provides ample support for any one theory to the exclusion of another. Let us be clear about what we are saying and not saying: we are not saying that the biological theories have been disproven. We are not saying that the psychological theories have been proven. Neither are we urging cynical attitudes toward the hard work of science; we have made tremendous advances in our understanding of persons and how we function, but the jury is still out on these complicated questions of causation. We are saying that the scientific evidence about causation is simply inconclusive at this time.

Further, readers must understand that we may not have to choose between particular theories within the nature or nurture clusters, between nature and nurture as general categories, or even between nature, nurture and human freedom. It may be more accurate and more helpful to pursue an "interactionist hypothesis" where various psychological, environmental and biological factors, together with human choice, contribute to different degrees that vary from person to person (see table 3.3).

Based on our understanding of the present research, we are both inclined to embrace a "weighted interactionist hypothesis." This is the same sort of conclusion toward which the famous sexologist John Money was inclined when he stated that "there is no human evidence that prenatal hormonalization alone, independently of postnatal history, inexorably preordains . . . [homosexuality]. Rather, neonatal antecedents may facilitate a homosexual . . . orientation, provided the postnatal deter-

---

[69]Byne and Parsons, "Human Sexual Orientation," p. 228. In fact, some scientists embrace psychosocial models for homosexuality, reject biological theories altogether and advocate for new ways to promote socially constructed sexualities. For some, the research may only be cited to support a position that is embraced for sociopolitical and moral valuative reasons rather than in an attempt to find out what is true about same-sex attraction.

1	2	3	4	Categories
Biological Antecedents +/−	Childhood Experiences +/−	Environmental Influences +/−	Adult Experiences +/−	Homosexual
				——— Bisexual ———
	Childhood Experiences +/−	Environmental Influences +/−	Adult Experiences +/−	Heterosexual

Table 3.3. Weighted interactionist hypothesis for experiences of same-sex attraction. The four major domains cover a broad array of influences. For example, biological antecedents may include genetic and prenatal hormonal, just as childhood experiences could include childhood sexual trauma, gender atypical play, and poor parental relationships. The more positive (+) a person is on factors associated with same-sex attraction in adulthood, the more likely to adopt a homosexual orientation; likewise, a negative (−) experience, i.e., not having that experience or predisposing factor, means less weight given toward an overall homosexual adaptation. These are weighted in that not everyone's experience will carry the same weight in facilitating a homosexual orientation.

minants in the social and communicational history are also facilitative."[70] Money's conclusion about prenatal hormones applies to genes and brain structure as well.

This means we believe that an individual person's experience of same-sex attraction will be related to a host of interrelated factors. We have discussed in detail two major categories of influence: biological influences and psychological (early childhood) influences such as parent-child relationships and childhood sexual abuse. We would add to these at least two other major categories of experience that might lead a person to experience same-sex attraction or identify himself as gay or herself lesbian later in life. These other two categories of influence are other environmental influences (such as peer group influences, same-sex experimentation and early sexual debut) and adult experiences (for example, willful or purposeful experimentation with same-sex behavior and subculture disinhibition).

It is important to note, however, that each individual who experiences same-sex attraction or later identifies as gay or lesbian will have unique predispositions and experiences that contribute more or less to that person's emerging sexual identity. In other words, these predispositions and experiences are *weighted differently* for each individual. For example, biological influences may exert greater power on average for males than females (or for a particular male more so than another male). These weighted predispositions and experiences can also be *cumulative*, so that early childhood experiences may influence one person more so than another, in part because of biological antecedents, and in part because of the nature, extent and duration of the childhood experiences. Each of these unique influences and experiences can provide a "push" in the direction of homosexuality, though no one experience or push "causes" a person to be homosexual. So a person with no predisposition to homosexuality and no experiences of trauma or difficulties relating to a primary caregiver can still engage in same-sex behavior, but the likelihood of primary identification as exclusively homosexual is low.

Two brief speculative examples may serve to illustrate this point.

1. George might be born as the second son with a moderately strong

---

[70]John Money, "Sin, Sickness, or Status? Homosexual Gender Identity and Psychoneuroendocrinology," *American Psychologist* 42 (1987): 397.

biological "push" toward being effeminate. His father, a "man's man," cannot relate to his second son's gentle temperament and so develops a more intense bond yet with his rough-and-tumble older son. His mother, sensing his lack of "standing" with his father, reaches out in compassion and intensifies her friendship with George as he grows. George struggles as a young man with feeling like he doesn't quite fit in, a feeling that he cannot even articulate clearly. These feelings leave him vulnerable, however, as he is flattered by the attention (attention that quickly turns sexual) from an older boy at the music camp that George attends at age thirteen. By the time he is fifteen, George has clearly begun to think of himself as gay.

2. Tanya is born without biological disposition toward homosexuality at all. Sadly, her parents divorce at age five, and she witnesses her mother go through a horrible time of adjusting to being single. Her mother relies on alcohol and brief flings with men to get her through this time. Her mother marries impulsively when Tanya is nine. Her new "blended family" includes a thirteen-year-old stepbrother who surreptitiously begins ever-escalating sexual abuse of Tanya. The marriage explodes by the time Tanya is fourteen, but deep damage has been done. Tanya, in her loneliness and confusion, marries impulsively at age nineteen, resulting in an unsatisfactory marriage that further confirms her deep distrust of men. When she finally feels she is getting her life straightened out in graduate school, she finds herself drawn to a woman who shares her distrust of men and who seems capable of meeting her emotional and sexual needs. The relationship turns intensely emotional and sexual. Tanya "discovers" that she is really a lesbian.

Such case studies prove nothing; anyone can tell a convincing story. But they do illustrate that multiple "causal forces" can work together to bring a person to a particular point in life.

Researchers are just exploring the tip of the iceberg in studying each major category of influence. Perhaps future research will provide greater clarity than what is available at present. We can see no compelling reason, though, to believe that any one theory will sufficiently explain such a diverse and complex phenomenon as human homosexuality.

Formal Relevance of Research to the Moral Debate

After this long review of what "science says," we turn as promised to the next question: What is the formal relevance of research on the origins of homosexuality to the moral debate in the church? What if future research suggests the presence of powerful causal influences, be they psychological/familial or biological? There are really two questions to answer. First, if there were mounting research on causal influences, would these psychological/familial or biological influences render human choice utterly irrelevant to the formation of sexual orientation? Second, would such findings have any direct bearing on the moral debate about what a person does with these sexual feelings?

To answer the first question, we have said before that there appear to be a variety of factors that provide a push in the direction of homosexuality for some persons, but there is *no evidence that this "push" renders human choice utterly irrelevant.* We can agree with Byne and Parsons, who argue that human choice can be accurately viewed as one of the factors influencing the development of sexual orientation, but that this "is not meant to imply that one consciously decides one's sexual orientation. Instead, sexual orientation is assumed to be shaped and reshaped by a cascade of choices made in the context of changing circumstances in one's life and enormous social and cultural pressures,"[71] and, we would add, in the context of considerable predispositions toward certain types of preferences.

Christian thinkers should reject a false and easy dichotomy between free choice and utterly determined causation. There are actually gradations in our capacities to make choices. A little child does not have the capacity to exercise the kind of patience and self-restraint that a mature adult can manifest; the child must be trained to be able to exhibit such patterns. On a different note, the person who thoughtlessly cultivates bad habits is actually slowly undermining his or her capacity to make other, better choices as the sheer momentum of destructive patterns gains power over his or her life. And perhaps, as Baumrind[72] and others have argued, for some people sexual proclivities really are their chosen sexual preference, as adult converts to lesbianism seem to exemplify.

Many are most troubled by the concept of "choice" when it is linked

---

[71]Ibid., p. 228.
[72]D. Baumrind, "Commentary on Sexual Orientation: Research and Social Policy Implications," *Developmental Psychology* 31 (1995): 130-36.

to "genetic causation." We are used to thinking of genes as causing us to have things like brown eyes or wavy hair, and choice has little to do with such characteristics. But behavior genetics has produced abundant evidence of genetic influences that clearly do not render human choice irrelevant. One study of the correlations between television viewing of adopted children and their adoptive and biological parents produced evidence of "significant genetic influence on individual differences in children's television viewing."[73] In other words, the television viewing patterns of adopted children had more in common with that of their genetic/biological parents than of their adopted parents! This finding helps to put the genetic evidence into perspective. All of us would reject the notion that our genes make us sit for a certain number of hours in front of a television screen, but what our genes may do is give us a predisposition of some sort (sedentary tendencies?) that would make the choice to view television more or less appealing to certain people. What may be inherited, then, is how much we are prone to like television viewing over other things. The husband who uses this as an excuse to be a couch potato ("But honey, my genes are making me watch *Monday Night Football!*"), however, is on thin ice.

This helps us answer a pressing question that is a corollary of the issue of choice: "Does the finding of any influence from nonchosen variables make choice irrelevant and thus sin disappear?" This question has been expressed directly in the church debates as an assertion: *"Although the evidence is still inconclusive, if the recent discoveries prove accurate, the individual does not have the free choice that is an essential to sinful behavior."*[74]

The answer, the rebuttal, to this claim should now be clear, and in answering it, we are addressing the second question of whether research in this area has any formal bearing on the moral status of homosexual behavior. *Science has not eliminated responsibility for sexual behavior.* None of the research cited in this chapter paints homosexual persons as some sort

---

[73]R. Plomin, R. Corley, J. C. DeFries and D. W. Fulker, "Individual Differences in Television Viewing in Early Childhood: Nature as Well as Nurture," *Psychological Science* 1 (1990): 371.

[74]A letter from William P. Thompson to Vernon B. Van Bruggen, October 15, 1993, cited in Sylvia Thorson-Smith, *Reconciling the Broken Silence: The Church in Dialogue on Gay and Lesbian Issues* (Louisville, Ky.: Christian Education Program Area of the Congregational Ministry Division, Presbyterian Church USA., 1993), p. 30.

of subhuman robots who can make no real choices about how they behave.

The church's moral concern is not fundamentally with homosexual orientation, no matter how it develops. We do not fully understand what a sexual orientation is, but from a moral perspective, from a Christian perspective, it may best be understood as one among the many ways in which we humans, sinful and fallen as we are, are inclined to lean toward choices and patterns that do not bring honor to God.

The church's moral concern is with what an individual does with his or her experiences of same-sex attraction. Only in the case of extreme biological determination at the level of individual acts would moral culpability be seen as obliterated. Homosexual persons are not subhuman robots whose acts are predetermined. They are moral agents who inherit tendencies from biology and environment, and who share in shaping their character by the responses they make to their life situations. Like all persons, they must ask, "This is what I want to do, but is it what I should do?" The existence of inclinations or predispositions does not erase the need for moral evaluation of those inclinations.

Finally, we want to briefly return to a matter raised earlier. We quoted McNeil, who stated "Only a sadistic God would create hundreds of thousands of humans to be inherently homosexual and then deny them the right to sexual intimacy."[75] To this we must respond, "Who made sexual intimacy a right?" Rather than a right, Scripture would seem to paint sexual chastity an obligation for those who, for whatever reason, do not find themselves married (whether those reasons are an unwanted divorce, lack of available partners, death of a spouse or because of a religious vow). Homosexual persons have the same capacities for all other sorts of intimacy other than erotic sexual intimacy that serve to sustain and nourish us. But more on this in chapter six.

Summary

☐ Proponents for change caricature traditionalists as arguing that homosexuality is a "perverse lifestyle choice" rather than an "innate characteristic." By framing the debate in these terms, any scientific evidence in support of a more robust view of homosexual orientation as an enduring,

---

[75]J. J. McNeil, "Homosexuality: Challenging," p. 53.

universal characteristic, perhaps tied to various biological antecedents, will make the caricature of traditionalists look scientifically uninformed.

☐ Gender nonconformity in childhood seems to be related to adult experiences of homosexuality. There appears to be evidence in favor of both psychological/environmental theories and genetic and prenatal hormonal theories for the origins of same-sex attraction.

☐ Many of the psychological/environmental theories for the origins of same-sex attraction are grounded in theories that implicate the parent/child relationship or other environmental factors such as childhood sexual trauma. The considerable amount of research supporting these theories has been largely ignored (rather than refuted) because of recent attempts to find support for a biological theory.

☐ The biological theories (genetic/prenatal hormonal) receive much more attention today. Some of the studies cited to support these theories have not been replicated, have been of small sample sizes or have serious methodological flaws. The best recent study of genetic causation, the new Bailey study,[76] suggests that genetics may not be a significant causal factor. More research is needed in these areas to further our understanding of the viability of the biological theories for the origins of same-sex attraction.

☐ Many experts in this area agree that an "interactionist hypothesis" is probably the best explanation for the origins of same-sex attraction.

☐ The church's moral concern is not with homosexual orientation but with what an individual does with his or her experiences of same-sex attraction.

Discussion Questions

1. How many different theories have you heard as to the "cause" of homosexuality?

2. How helpful do you think animal studies are to our understanding of human sexuality?

3. Is it possible that because there are many different kinds of experiences of same-sex attraction, that there may be many contributing influences, and that some of these vary from person to person?

4. How relevant are studies on the origins of same-sex attraction to the moral debate in the church?

---

[76]Bailey, Dunne, and Martin, "Genetic and Environmental Influences."

4

Is Homosexuality a Psychopathology?

The crucial issue in determining whether or not homosexuality per se is to be regarded as a mental disorder is not the etiology of the condition, but its consequences and the definition of mental disorder. A significant proportion of homosexuals are apparently satisfied with their sexual orientation, show no significant signs of manifest psychopathology (unless homosexuality, by itself, is considered psychopathology), and are able to function socially and occupationally with no impairment. If one uses the criteria of distress or disability, homosexuality per se is not a mental disorder.
—*DIAGNOSTIC AND STATISTICAL MANUAL
OF MENTAL DISORDERS*, 3RD EDITION

*S*everal *years ago Mark was speaking to members of a small church* about the topic of homosexuality. In the course of reviewing the research on elevated rates of sexual partners among homosexual men, some of the members of the congregation grew noticeably uncomfortable and asked several questions about the findings. One or two people cited "evidence" in the form of anecdotes: friends they know who are gay or lesbian and who to the best of their knowledge do not have multiple partners or a string of partners that would suggest abnormal behavior. Later in the presentation, when the topic of biological evidences for the predisposition to same-sex attraction was raised, these same members of the congregation nodded in approval of the research. The evening began to take the form of a daytime talk show, with people voicing approval for some research ("Amen!" to research implicating biology in the formation of same-sex attraction) and then rejecting other studies out of hand ("No way!" to research on nonexclusivity among homosexual persons).

Later that same year Mark was presenting some of the scientific research to a much more conservative Christian church. In that setting most people were uncomfortable with hearing about the possibility that biology might in some indirect way contribute to predispositions to same-sex attraction. But members of the more conservative church were more capable of hearing about research on elevated rates of depression or suicidality or increased nonmonogamy among homosexual persons. The reverse of the pattern observed in the first church was noted: "Amen!" to research on depression, suicidality and nonmonogamy, and "No way!" to research on predispositions that might be linked to biology.

These experiences point to one of the problems in reviewing and presenting research, especially research on a controversial topic like homosexuality. We often come to the research with our biases. Sometimes these biases make it difficult to *see* the findings for what they actually are. Perhaps this is nowhere more true than around the issue of whether homosexuality is a psychopathology or mental illness.

The short answer to the question, "Is homosexuality a psychopathology?" is no, if a person were to mean that the answer can be found by a quick look through the *Diagnostic and Statistical Manual of Mental Disorders; Fourth Edition* (DSM-IV) of the American Psychiatric Association. Homosexuality is not listed as a formal mental disorder in the DSM-IV, and hence it is not a "mental illness." But, as we will see in this chapter, answering the question, "Is homosexuality a psychopathology?" is much more complicated than simply checking a manual.

The Use of Science in Religious Documents

The view that homosexuality does not signal a mental illness, and in fact is judged to be a healthy lifestyle variant, is often cited in the mainline denominational literature as the basis for needed change in the traditional Christian stance toward homosexuality. As in the previous chapters some arguments are straightforward pronouncements about the health and morality of homosexuality, while other arguments are indirect claims based on a presentation of a caricature of traditionalists that is then denounced by an appeal to science.

If we return to Chandler Burr's chapter in a book promoting church dialogue on homosexuality, we read, "Five decades of psychiatric evidence demonstrates that homosexuality is nonpathological."[1] Burr implies that this brute fact should serve as an impetus to change church moral teaching.

Similarly, Sylvia Thorson-Smith, writing in a book promoting church dialogue on gay and lesbian issues, cites the famous Evelyn Hooker studies conducted in the 1950s (and which we will discuss at length later) and draws conclusions from that research:

> In 1956, psychologist Evelyn Hooker reported the findings of her ground-breaking study that demonstrated indistinguishable mental health profiles of heterosexual and gay men. Her study was followed by additional research showing that homosexuals "who do not regret their sexual orientation, and who can function effectively sexually and socially are no more distressed psychologically than are heterosexual men and women."[2]

Thorson draws dramatic implications from this assertion: she urges the church to (1) change its teaching on the moral status of homosexual behavior; (2) open all clerical offices to practicing homosexual clergy; (3) "acknowledge the homophobia in ourselves;" and (4) "welcome all persons, including lesbian, gay and bisexual persons, into the full life of the church at all levels including ordained office if so chosen."[3] So we see again an effort to draw moral conclusions directly from the "findings" of science.

Perhaps the clearest example of how proponents for change attempt to shape the moral debate based upon the findings of science comes from the following study group for a mainline church. In this study guide, scientific endorsements of homosexuality as a healthy sexual variant are followed by implications for the ethical arguments in the church:

> If it could be shown that homosexuality is generally a symptom of unmet emotional needs or difficulties in social adjustment, then this might point to problems in relating to God and other persons. But if that cannot generally be shown, homosexuality may be compatible with life in grace.[4]

---

[1]Chandler Burr, "Homosexuality and Biology," *Homosexuality in the Church: Both Sides of the Debate*, ed. Jeffrey S. Siker (Louisville, Ky: Westminster John Knox, 1993), p. 65.

[2]Sylvia Thorson-Smith, *Reconciling the Broken Silence: The Church in Dialogue on Gay and Lesbian Issues* (Louisville, Ky.: Christian Education Area of the Congregational Ministry Division, Presbyterian Church USA), p. 46.

[3]Ibid., pp. 98-99.

[4]United Methodist Church, General Council on Ministries, *Report of The Committee to Study*

The report went on to conclude:

> The scientific evidence is sufficient to support the contention that homo-
> sexuality is not pathological or otherwise an inversion, developmental fail-
> ure, or deviant form of life as such, but is rather a human variant, one that
> can be healthy and whole.[5]

The tone in these examples is that "everybody knows" that homosexuality is a normal human variation. Specific research findings are
not cited. Further, there is imbedded in this report a subtle caricature
of the traditionalists' view, the implication that they view same-sex
behavior as immoral *because* homosexuality is a psychopathology or
mental illness. To refute the caricature, proponents need only cite evidence that homosexuality is no longer a pathology and that "everybody knows" that homosexuality is just another viable option for
sexual expression.

Often, the caricature of the traditionalist position is more openly presented as scientifically naive or ignorant. In a draft of a pastoral teaching
of the House of Bishops to the Episcopal Church, the committee discusses eight "assumptions that should be challenged."[6] The third assumption is that "Gays and lesbians are psychologically 'sick,' " to which the
committee responds that

> researchers have failed to discern any demonstrable psychopathology in
> their homosexual samples, nor have they been able to differentiate homo-
> sexual from heterosexual subjects, suggesting that there is no greater
> pathology or tendency toward psychological maladjustment among homo-
> sexuals than heterosexuals.[7]

The committee is apparently making reference to the research by Evelyn Hooker and others, although the omission of actual research studies

---

Homosexuality to the General Council on Ministries of the United Methodist Church (Dayton,
Ohio: General Council of Ministries, 1991), p. 27.

[5]Ibid., p. 28.

[6]Committee A104sa of the House of Bishops, Episcopal Church in the United States of
America, *Continuing the Dialogue: A Pastoral Teaching of the House of Bishops to the Church as It
Considers Issues of Human Sexuality,* 5th draft (1994), pp. 42-46. Distributed to the bishops of
the ECUSA with a cover letter from the presiding bishop dated July 12, 1994, from the
Episcopal Church Center, New York.

[7]Ibid., p. 43.

presents a greater challenge to the Christian who would want to research the claims and assertions made in this resource book. Once it is established that the myth is foolish, traditionalists are made to look uninformed, naive or ignorant. It begins to look like traditionalists reject science altogether or at least have little regard for advancements in our scientific knowledge. But these appeals to science beg the question, "What *do* we actually know about homosexuality from the scientific research conducted to date?"

A Review of the Scientific Literature
It is widely known that in 1974 the full membership of the American Psychiatric Association (APA) followed the 1973 recommendation of its board by voting to remove homosexuality as a pathological psychiatric condition *as such* (or "in itself") from the DSM, which is the official reference book for diagnosing mental disorders in America (and through much of the world).[8] The removal of homosexuality from the DSM was in response to a majority vote of the APA. The original APA vote was called at a time of significant social change and was taken with unconventional speed that circumvented normal channels for consideration of the issues because of explicit threats from gay rights groups to disrupt APA conventions and research.[9]

However, it appears that in contrast to the results of the vote, the majority of the APA membership continued to view homosexuality as a pathology. A survey four years after the vote found that 69% of psychiatrists regarded homosexuality as a "pathological adaptation."[10] A much

---

[8]The removal was actually something that happened in stages. Homosexuality itself ceased to be classified as a psychiatric condition, a mental illness, with the 1974 vote. For a number of years, however, the diagnosis of "Ego-Dystonic Homosexuality" remained as a diagnostic category (see the DSM-III); this term referred to people who were homosexual and who regarded that sexual orientation as discordant with their ego or self-identity, alien to their deepest sense of who they were as a person. This category was then relegated to a subcategorization under "Sexual Disorders Not Otherwise Specified" in the DSM-III (revised), and then the word *ego-dystonic* was omitted entirely in the DSM-IV. What remains in DSM-IV in the "Sexual Disorders not Otherwise Specified" is mention of "persistent and marked distress about sexual orientation" (p. 249). There is also mention of sexual orientation as an "Identity Problem," which is listed as a V-Code.

[9]Ronald Bayer, *Homosexuality and American Psychiatry: The Politics of Diagnosis* (New York: Basic Books, 1981).

more recent survey suggests that the majority of psychiatrists around the world continue to view same-sex behavior as signaling mental illness.[11]

The removal of homosexuality from the DSM does not answer the thorny question of the morality of homosexual behavior, as we will discuss later. It also does not answer the question of whether or not homosexual orientation is "healthy." Removal of the diagnostic category from the DSM is not the same thing as an endorsement of homosexual orientation or lifestyle as healthy or wholesome, as the two surveys conducted since the APA vote would indicate. By analogy, a person can certainly be in a condition where he or she fails to manifest an identifiable physical disease, yet also fails to be an exemplar of health and fitness.

The removal of homosexuality from the DSM does not conclusively decide the issue of the pathological status of homosexuality. There is no absolute standard for judging normality or abnormality. Four empirical (or at least partially empirical) criteria are commonly used to define behavior patterns as abnormal:

☐ statistical infrequency

☐ personal distress

☐ maladaptiveness and

☐ deviation from social norms

Before we look at the research in each of these areas, we want to discuss the limitations or challenges of the research in this area.

Methodological Challenges

Perhaps more than in any area we have examined so far, deciding the question of whether or not homosexuality is pathological hinges on making valid generalizations about homosexuals as a group. To make such generalizations validly, you must have good information about the entire group. The major challenge that comes up again and again in making generalizeable statements about homosexuality is the challenge of finding a *sample* of homosexual persons that is representative of *all* homosexual persons.

The first major study that challenged the view that homosexuality was

---

[10]Bayer, *Homosexuality and American*, p. 167.

[11]American Psychiatric Association, "Psychiatrists' Views on Homosexuality," *Psychiatric News*, September 1993, a survey conducted by the APA's Office of International Affairs.

intrinsically abnormal was the study by psychologist Evelyn Hooker, who administered psychological tests on a group of "healthy" homosexuals and compared those results with results from a group of heterosexuals. To the surprise of the mental health establishment, skilled psychologists, who were trained to make such diagnoses, could not distinguish the heterosexuals from the homosexuals on the basis of their test results alone. By their test findings alone, this group of homosexuals appeared to be no different and had no worse problems then the heterosexuals. The prevailing wisdom at that time was that to be homosexual was to manifest obvious signs of pathology. Common wisdom dictated that the homosexuals should have obviously differed from the heterosexuals. Hooker's study challenged this commonplace asumption. In this study Hooker refuted the generalization that all homosexuals are manifestly disturbed. This study was the logical equivalent of refuting the judgment that "all women are intellectually inferior to men" by demonstrating that a select sample of intellectually gifted women performed as well as a sample of men on a math test.

But, as we mentioned above, Hooker's study is often interpreted as having accomplished much more. Remember the church document on human sexuality we cited earlier? It stated that researchers have been unable "to differentiate homosexual from heterosexual subjects, suggesting that there is no greater pathology or tendency toward psychological maladjustment among homosexuals than heterosexuals."[12]

Is this interpretation of Hooker's research accurate? No. We would argue that it is valid to say that the findings from Hooker's study demonstrated that *it is not the case that all homosexuals are manifestly disturbed*. But many popular reports suggest or give the impression that what Hooker's study has proven is that homosexuals are as emotionally healthy as heterosexuals, or that homosexuality per se is not psychopathological.

Logically and methodologically, her study neither proved that homosexu-

---

[12]House of Bishops to the Episcopal Church, *Continuing the Dialogue*, p. 52. Mental health professionals sometimes make similarly misleading (but less obviously inaccurate) statements: "In the 1960s, sociologist Evelyn Hooker gave a battery of tests to gay and straight volunteers who were not in therapy and found that there was no difference in the amount of pathology between the two. It was this study which helped lead to the declassification of homosexuality as a mental illness."; Mary Bart, "Counselors say conversion therapy claims are groundless and prejudicial," *Counseling Today* 40 (December 1998): 24-29.

als are as emotionally healthy as heterosexuals, nor did it prove that homosexuality per se is not pathological. In order to have adequately addressed either of these important claims, Hooker would have had to study a *representative* sample of homosexual persons. In Hooker's own words,

> It should also be stated at the outset that no assumptions are made about the random selection of either group [homosexual or heterosexual]. No one knows what a random sample of the homosexual population would be like; and even if one knew, it would be extremely difficult, if not impossible, to obtain one.[13]

What is not commonly understood is just how unusual the sample for Hooker's study was. In order to obtain her sample Hooker worked openly with pro-homosexual organizations in the mid-1950s to recruit a sample of well-adjusted homosexual persons. Further, she explicitly required of those in the study that they not be under psychiatric or psychological treatment (though it is not clear from her report if her recruits were not in therapy currently, at the time of recruitment for the study or had never been in therapy). We have no idea what percentage of homosexual persons utilized therapy in the 1950s, but a recent study found that 77.5% of lesbians (compared to 28.9% of heterosexual women) had been in therapy.[14] What makes this important? *Hooker's insistence on a sample where no one was in therapy may have made her study extraordinarily nonrepresentative of homosexuals.*

Samples that are not representative of the population you are studying are only a problem if certain types of claims are being investigated. If you are trying to answer the question "Are there any men who are good fathers?" then you do not need a representative sample of men but only need to sample men until you find a good father. If you are trying to answer the question "What percentage of all men are good fathers?" then you *must* have a representative sample of fathers or your answer will be invalid. The question Hooker was examining was like the first question: in response to the common understanding that "all homosexuals are dis-

---

[13]Evelyn Hooker, "The Adjustment of the Male Overt Homosexual," in *The Problem of Homosexuality in Modern Society,* ed. Hendrick M. Ruitenbeek (New York: E. P. Dutton, 1963), p. 142.

[14]J. Bradford, Caitlin Ryan and Esther D. Rothblum, "National Lesbian Care Survey: Implications for Mental Health Care," *Journal of Consulting and Clinical Psychology* 62 (1994): 228-42.

turbed," Hooker asked the question "Is there a group of homosexuals who are not noticeably more disturbed than heterosexuals?" Hooker did refute the claim that *all homosexuals are manifestly disturbed* in a similar way that one "conversion" of a homosexual to heterosexuality refutes the absolute claim that homosexuality cannot be changed. But she did *not* prove that homosexuals are as emotionally healthy as heterosexuals, nor that homosexuality per se is not pathological.

We are still left with the question, "Is homosexuality abnormal?" To answer this question we will now review the research on each of the four criteria for defining pathology to further our understanding of whether homosexuality is abnormal.

Statistical Infrequency

We mentioned in the chapter on prevalence rates that a lifelong exclusive or near-exclusive homosexual orientation is not common. Perhaps 2% of the combined male and female population manifest this pattern. Compare this percentage to the estimated lifetime incidence rates of some other major psychopathological disorders. In comparison, the prevalence of homosexuality is much less frequent than such common disorders as phobias (14.3%) and alcohol abuse and dependence (13.8%), about as frequent as some disorders that are less common, as is the case with panic (1.6%) and schizophrenia (1.5%), and much more frequent than somatization disorders (0.1%).[15]

In comparison to these prevalence rates, homosexuality is not so common as to be eliminated as a possible pathology on frequency alone. But even with a lower estimate of homosexuality than public perception might indicate, we have no absolute cutoff for judging pathology by frequency or infrequency alone; there is no rule stating that a pattern cannot be judged a pathology if it is manifested by more than X% of the population.

Personal Distress

Psychopathology is often accompanied by personal distress, as is the case with depressive disorders and sexual dysfunctions. However, personal

---

[15]Lee N. Robins, Ben Z. Locke and Darrel A. Regier, "An Overview of Psychiatric Disorders in America," in *Psychiatric Disorders in America: The Epidemiological Catchment Area Study*, ed. Lee N. Robins and Darrel A. Regier (New York: Free Press, 1991), p. 343.

distress is not a necessary aspect of psychopathology. Some problems that we all recognize as pathological are also characterized by patterns of denial and minimization of distress, as is the case with some experiences of alcoholism or drug addiction.[16] Think of the alcoholic who refuses treatment and adamantly claims to have his or her drinking under control. The alcoholic may not report personal distress, and some alcoholics will be able to manage their various responsibilities, at least for the time being, which is why some professionals refer to them as "functional alcoholics." Some disorders, such as Antisocial Personality Disorder, are actually characterized at a fundamental level by a failure to be distressed about the patterns of behavior one manifests.

With homosexuality the claim is often made that "there is no evidence of higher rates of emotional instability or psychiatric illness among homosexuals than among heterosexuals."[17] This claim has been made so often that it has taken on the status of a truth that "everybody knows"; however, the factual basis for this assertion is debatable.

The two most frequently cited studies in support of this claim are the studies by Hooker[18] and by Saghir and Robins.[19] As we discussed earlier, the study conducted by Hooker proved that a select sample of homosexuals were no more distressed than (and could not be distinguished based on psychological testing from) a heterosexual sample. We also demonstrated that because of the nonrepresentativeness of her sample, she *did not in fact prove* the conclusion that Masters and his colleagues claim.

---

[16]This is actually a point of some discussion. The revision of DSM from DSM-III to DSM-IV included the necessity of having some conditions be personally distressing. For example, although pedophilia used to be diagnosed as a mental illness apart from whether the pedophile was distressed by his or her inclinations, the current diagnostic criteria requires that a person experience personal distress. It is conceivable that a person could be sexually attracted to children and not meet the current diagnostic criteria for pedophilia given the changes in DSM-IV. Some see this change as a disturbing trend in a society that is trying hard not to offend interest groups.

[17]William Masters, Virginia Johnson and Robert Kolodny, *Human Sexuality*, 4th ed. (Glenview, Ill.: Scott, Foresman, 1992), p. 394.

[18]Evelyn Hooker, "The Adjustment of the Male Overt Homosexual," *Journal of Projective Techniques* 21 (1957): 18-31; Evelyn Hooker, "The Adjustment of the Male Overt Homosexual," in *The Problem of Homosexuality in Modern Society*, ed. Hendrik M. Ruitenbeek (New York: E. P. Dutton, 1963).

[19]Marcel T. Saghir and Eli Robins, *Male and Female Homosexuality: A Comprehensive Investigation* (Baltimore: Williams and Wilkins, 1973).

The Saghir and Robins study has the same limitations as Hooker's. Their sample was also selected to minimize or exclude psychopathology. The authors note that their subjects were recruited from "homophile organizations,"[20] and presumably there was some self-selection operating given the announced objective of the project as the study of emotionally stable homosexual persons. They explicitly set out to recruit healthy homosexuals. After volunteering, subjects were further screened and excluded on the basis of prior psychiatric hospitalization. Interestingly, 14% of the male homosexual sample and 7% of the female homosexual sample were excluded from the study because of prior psychiatric hospitalizations, yet none of the heterosexuals who volunteered (the control group sample) were excluded on that basis.

The best estimate we can obtain of lifetime psychiatric hospitalization comes from Robins, Locke and Regier,[21] who report a lifetime prevalence of diagnosable mental disorder for women of 30% and report that on an annual basis only 2.4% of those with a diagnosable disorder are hospitalized for a psychiatric disorder.[22] If we double this estimate of hospitalization to be conservative in our estimate and to compensate for the higher psychiatric hospitalization rates for women, these findings would suggest that no more than 1.5% of the American female population is hospitalized for psychiatric reasons in their lifetime (30% x 5%). This is probably an overestimate because many of the psychopathologies included in the study by Robins et al. (e.g., phobias, generalized anxiety, dysthymia) infrequently result in hospitalization. So while Saghir and Robins conclude that the homosexual population experiences no increased incidence of psychopathology, their study must be interpreted within the context of their having screened out previously hospitalized individuals that, if included, would suggest a hospitalization rate for homosexuals approximately 450% higher than the general population, which in turn would suggest a conclusion opposite of that stated. Ironically, then, this study, which is touted as proving that homosexuals are just as healthy as a group as heterosexuals, actually provides evidence suggesting higher rates of psychiatric disorder among homosexuals. A

---

[20]Ibid., p. 6.
[21]Robins, Locke and Regier, "Overview of Psychiatric Disorders," p. 333.
[22]Ibid., p. 341.

recent study provides similar evidence. Bradford and her colleagues reported[23] findings from the "National Lesbian Health Care Survey." They minimized differences between homosexual and heterosexual women. The authors argued that the two groups were similar except for elevated use of alcohol and drugs and elevated use of counseling for lesbians (77.5% for the lesbian sample). But a closer look at their results tells a different tale. The data actually suggest that the lesbians studied experience elevated incidence of a number of significant problems.

The authors reported that 37% of the lesbians surveyed had experienced significant depression in their lifetime, that 11% were experiencing depression at the time of the survey, and that 11% were currently in treatment for their depression. The best estimate[24] for the general female population are 10.2% lifetime incidence of major depression, 3.1% current major depression, and probably less than 1% obtaining treatment for that depression in the year before the survey. The lesbian sample actually appears to experience significantly more depression.

Related to depression, Bradford and colleagues reported that 57% of the lesbians surveyed had experienced thoughts about suicide in their lifetime and that 18% had attempted suicide at least once. The best estimates for the general population are that 33% of women report lifetime "death thoughts" (a category much milder than thoughts about suicide, as it included answering yes to having "thought a lot about death" at any point in life, something that you can do when a grandparent dies), while the frequency of suicide attempts was so infrequent that it was not reported.[25]

Finally, Bradford and colleagues reported that 30% of the lesbians surveyed currently abused alcohol more than once a month, 8% abused marijuana more than once a month and 2% abused cocaine, tranquilizers or stimulants more than once a month. In contrast, Robins and Regier[26] estimated for the general population that 4.6% of women had abused alcohol in their lifetime and 1% in the last month, while 4.4% reported lifetime abuse of marijuana and less than 1% reported current abuse and abuse of other substances was very infrequent. These comparisons are

[23]Bradford, Ryan and Rothblum, "National Lesbian Health Care Survey," pp. 228-42.
[24]Robins and Regier, *Psychiatric Disorders*, tables 4.3 (p. 59) and 13.5 (p. 341).
[25]Ibid., table 4.7 (p. 63).
[26]Ibid., tables 5.1 (p. 85) and 6.4 (p. 123).

consistent in suggesting over 300% increases in incidence of serious personal distress among lesbians.

Objective assessment of other research suggests a similar pattern. Studies have found higher rates of depression and loneliness among male homosexuals, as well as "more paranoia and psychosomatic symptoms."[27] Further, 18% of white homosexual males (like the 18% of lesbians) reported attempting suicide at least once, compared to a much lower rate among heterosexual respondents.[28] In addition, Kus[29] reported elevated substance abuse rates among homosexual males.

We would also like to discuss the findings from two recent studies of the relationship between homosexuality and psychopathology. Both studies are stronger methodologically than most of the previous studies, although there are still limitations to these findings. The first study[30] is of 1,007 (of the original 1,265) New Zealanders (79.6% of those who were originally studied) who were followed through childhood as a birth cohort until they reached age twenty-one. Those who were identified as gay, lesbian or bisexual were at increased risks of major depression (odds ratio of 4.0 as compared to their heterosexual cohort), generalized anxiety disorder (odds ratio of 2.8), conduct disorder (odds ration of 3.8), nicotine dependence (odds ratio of 5.0), substance abuse or dependence (odds ratio of 1.9), suicidal ideation (odds ratio of 5.4) and suicidal attempts (odds ratio of 6.2).

Findings from the second more recent and more sophisticated study[31] on the association between homosexuality and psychopathology adds

---

[27]Alan P. Bell and Martin S. Weinberg, *Homosexualities: A Study of Diversity Among Men and Women* (New York: Simon & Schuster, 1978), p. 207.

[28]Ibid., p. 450. On suicidality among homosexual persons, see K. Erwin, "Interpreting the Evidence: Competing Paradigms and the Emergence of Lesbian and Gay Suicide as a 'Social Fact,' " *International Journal of Health Services* 23 (1993): 437-53.

[29]Robert J. Kus, "Alcoholism and Non-Acceptance of Gay Self: The Critical Link," *Journal of Homosexuality* 15 (1988): 25-41.

[30]Donald M. Ferguson, L. John Horwood and Annette L. Beautrais, "Is Sexual Orientation Related to Mental Health Problems and Suicidality in Young People?" *Archives of General Psychiatry* 56 (1999): 876-80.

[31]Richard Herrell, Jack Goldberg, William R. True, Visvanathan Ramakrishnan, Michael Lyons, Seth Eisen and Ming T. Tsuang, "Sexual Orientation and Suicidality: A Co-Twin Control Study in Adult Men," *Archives of General Psychiatry* 56 (1999): 867-74. The limitation to both of these more recent studies has to do with definitions of homosexual orientation (where both studies defined homosexuality as same-sex behavior in adulthood) and the failure to distinguish the experiences of male homosexuals and female homosexuals.

additional support to the hypothesis that homosexual persons are at greater risk for suicidality. The study was of 103 male twin pairs from the Vietnam Era Twin Registry in Illinois. Using the widely used Diagnostic Interview Schedule, elevations were reported for homosexual twins on four lifetime symptoms of suicidality (thoughts about death, wanting to die, thoughts about committing suicide and suicide attempts).[32]

Clearly some behaviors that suggest distress are more common among homosexuals. Still, it cannot be generally concluded that *all* homosexuals experience personal distress, nor can it be concluded that such distress is an *inevitable* part of the homosexual experience. Most homosexuals in the Bell and Weinberg study (which was not a random sample) did not regret being homosexual and were not judged to exhibit psychopathological symptoms. But this conclusion begs the question of whether they are, on average, more disposed than the heterosexual population to experience distress. All of the available empirical evidence would seem to point in that direction. It was thus for good reason that Baumrind, speaking only of gay and lesbian adolescents, remarked that "non-heterosexual youths manifest many symptoms of distress and problem behavior peculiar to, or exacerbated by, their lifestyles."[33]

We should note too that some pro-gay authors do not deny these indications of elevated distress. They move the argument, perhaps rightly so (at least in part), in a different direction. Perhaps, they suggest, distress is not the result of homosexuality itself, but the result of the way *society* treats homosexuals; perhaps elevated levels of distress among homosexuals are a reality but occur not because of any discomfort inherent to the orientation itself but rather in response to the interaction of gays and lesbians with a rejecting and punitive society. They liken these responses to those of other persecuted or rejected minority groups. Although this explanation is a post hoc interpretation of research, there is an important point here: few heterosexuals know the stress of living under persecution for their sexual feelings, and social hostility toward homosexuals is

---

[32]The specific findings were that homosexual orientation was associated with thoughts about death (odd ratio of 4.4), wanting to die (odds ratio of 4.1), suicidal ideation (odds ratio of 6.5), any suicidal symptoms (odds ratio of 5.1); see Herrell et al., "Sexual Orientation and Suicidality," p. 870, table 1.

[33]Diana Baumrind, "Commentary on Sexual Orientation: Research and Social Policy Implications," *Developmental Psychology* 31 (1995): 133.

bound to be an influencing factor in any measure of emotional stability.

Maladaptiveness

A behavior pattern or characteristic is "adaptive" when it is constructive, helpful, healthy and contributes to the person moving in a valued direction. If you are in college and value academic success, good study skills and self-discipline are adaptive, while alcohol abuse or learning disabilities are maladaptive. Maladaptiveness refers to behavior or characteristics that sabotage rather than abet a person's moving in a positive, healthy direction.

Maladaptiveness can only be judged against some standard of "adaptiveness." We share many common judgments of what is adaptive, and by logical extension, what is maladaptive. It is maladaptive to kill yourself, to be addicted to heroin, to hallucinate or be psychotic, to be unable to hold a job and contribute constructively to society and so forth.

But any standard of adaptiveness can be challenged: Is success at work or high income or relational stability or even the absence of self-injurious behavior really an utterly reliable standard of adaptiveness? Lurking behind every definition of adaptiveness and its opposite is a hidden, implicit model of wholeness and health, a vision of what constitutes a "good life." As we write this chapter, a white supremacist has just murdered and wounded a number of people and then committed suicide. Maladaptive behavior? Well, the murderer's primary racist mentor is refusing to condemn the assaults, calling the shooter a martyr and saying that the killings may have been necessary to wake up the "white race." To call the behavior and character of the murderer maladaptive, we must hold values that say that murder is wrong, that other races are people too, that hate is a disorder of the soul and so forth. Were the actions of Adolf Hitler maladaptive; or better, would they have been judged maladaptive in hindsight if he had won? What of the homeless person who says that he does not value jobs or relationships or the esteem of society but just wants to wander and be left alone?

There is a hidden dimension to judgments of adaptiveness: such judgments are always made against the backdrop of values and assumptions about what constitutes "good" for human life. And it is in the area of these judgments that different moral and religious ideologies often creep into the very fabric of our supposedly empirical, scientific psychology (and hence our earlier qualification about the criteria for what counts as abnormal as "partially" empirical).

So is homosexuality adaptive or maladaptive? The elevated rates of depression, substance abuse and suicide challenge the adaptiveness of homosexuality. Alternatively, not every homosexual contends with depression, substance abuse or suicidal thoughts. Moreover, the educational and vocational success, not to mention the recent political ascendancy of gay and lesbian concerns, might be seen as supporting the adaptiveness of this orientation.

Some early challenges to the adaptiveness of homosexuality were biological and focused upon the fact that homosexual sex was nonreproductive. If propelling genetic material into future generations is the point of all life, as the strict Darwinian must argue,[34] homosexuality would seem to be maladaptive. This view is not often voiced today, as sociobiologists now suggest that under some circumstances (such as overpopulation) homosexuality can contribute to overall enhancement of the human species by having a subpopulation removed from contributing to further propagation.[35] The AIDS epidemic has given pause to some regarding the biological adaptiveness of male homosexuality, since anal sex and some of the rougher, "high-tech" sexual practices of the gay subculture are such efficient methods for the spread of many sexually transmitted diseases.[36]

---

[34]Robert Wright, *The Moral Animal: The New Science of Evolutionary Psychology* (New York: Pantheon Books, 1994). Interestingly, to the extent that Christians view procreation as an essential part of "normal sex" (as the Roman Catholic Church teaches; see also our argument about the purposes of sexual intercourse in the final chapter), this may be an area of agreement between Darwinians and some Christians.

[35]Herbert A. Simon, "A Mechanism for Social Selection and Successful Altruism," *Science* 250 (1990): 1665-68.

[36]See a discussion of this and related material in Thomas Schmidt, *Straight and Narrow? Compassion and Clarity in the Homosexuality Debate* (Downers Grove, Ill.: InterVarsity Press, 1995). Kalichman suggests that the number of people infected with HIV through heterosexual contact quadrupled between 1989 and 1995, but the overall numbers are still disproportionately low compared to "men who have sex with men" (which is the official category used by the Centers for Disease Control and Prevention). At the end of 1997 heterosexual contact accounted for 58,884 out of 641,086 (9%) cumulative AIDS cases, while "men who have sex with men" accounted for 309,247 (48%) of the cumulative AIDS cases. See Seth C. Kalichman, *Answering Your Questions about AIDS* (Washington, D.C.: American Psychological Association); Centers for Disease Control and Prevention, *The HIV/AIDS Surveillance Report*, p. 9. Available online at <www.cdc.gov/hiv/stats/hivsur92.pdf>.

Many Christian ethicists, including some who are pro-gay, express a concern for monogamy. Traditionalists reserve their approval for heterosexual monogamy, while the gay-affirming ethicists promote monogamy regardless of the genders of partners. They argue that lifelong faithfulness to one partner, or least faithfulness to the partner currently committed to, is a moral good. This ethical concern would lead us to examine relational stability and fidelity as one important dimension of maladaptiveness, though this concern might be seen as peculiarly or parochially Christian.

Although it appears that lesbians show a greater capacity to form long-term relationships in a manner comparable to that of heterosexuals, male homosexuals as a population show a greatly reduced capacity for or propensity toward such relationships and a clear propensity for promiscuous behavior. A nonrandom but large sample of gay men (taken in San Francisco in the late 1970s) showed that only 10% of the respondents could be classified as existing in "close coupled" relationships, and these relationships in turn could only be characterized as "relatively monogamous" or "relatively less promiscuous."[37] In the same study 28% of white homosexual males reported having had 1,000 or more lifetime homosexual partners by the time they were interviewed, while only 17% reported having had fewer than 50 homosexual partners (thus 83% of white homosexual males had sexual relations with 50 or more partners in their lifetimes). In addition, 79% of white homosexual males reported that more than half of their sexual partners were strangers.[38] This was not a "typical sample" (if there is such a thing) of homosexual men; it was drawn from the San Francisco area at the very height of the celebration of that gay community of its freedom from the restraints of puritanical, middle class values, and before the AIDS epidemic struck (and it was precisely during this time that the HIV virus was being silently and efficiently spread).

A more recent study provided much less dramatic estimates from a

---

Although AIDS is not a "gay disease," it is clearly disproportionately represented among men who have sex with men given the low prevalence rates of homosexual men discussed in chapter two of this book. Recent attention has also turned to lesbians, who are at greater risk than was previously thought, primarily because lesbian and bisexual women who do have sex with men tend to be intimate with bisexual men. See R. A. Clay, "HIV Risk Among Lesbians is Higher than Most Realize," *APA Monitor*, February 1997, p. 28. Available online at <www.apa.org/monitor/feb97/lesbian.html>.

[37]Bell and Weinberg, *Homosexualities: A Study*, p. 346.

[38]Ibid., p. 308.

small but representative sample of homosexuals. In their nationally representative sample, Laumann[39] and his colleagues found that on average gay men reported 42.8 lifetime sexual partners compared to 16.5 for heterosexual men, a 260% increase. Lesbians reported almost exactly 100% more partners than the average heterosexual woman (9.4 lifetime partners for lesbians; 4.6 lifetime partners for heterosexual women).

David McWhirter and Andrew Mattison conducted a nonrandom study[40] of 156 stable, committed male homosexual couples. They found that none of the over 100 couples that had been together for more than five years had been sexually monogamous or exclusive. The authors, themselves a gay couple, argued that for male couples, sexual monogamy is a passing stage of internalized homophobia, and that many homosexual males distinguish between emotional fidelity and sexual exclusivity. What matters for male couples, according to McWhirter and Mattison, is emotional, not physical, faithfulness.[41]

Similarly, Deenen, Gijs and van Naerssen[42] studied 156 gay couples and reported that the majority of partners in the study (62%) had had sexual encounters outside of the relationship in the year before the survey. The average number of extrarelational sexual partners for each member of the gay couples in the year before the survey was 7.1.

So we are left with the question of whether the capacity to form and maintain stable monogamous sexual relationships is an essential adaptive capacity. If so, then real difficulties for male homosexuals emerge. If the psychological community deemphasizes relational stability among its criteria of adaptiveness or healthy emotional adjustment,[43] then promiscuity in the male homosexual community does not constitute maladjustment.

---

[39]Edward O. Laumann, John H. Gagron, Robert T. Michael and Stuart Michaels, *The Social Organization of Sexuality* (London and Chicago: University of Chicago Press, 1994), p. 315.

[40]David P. McWhirter and Andrew M. Mattison, *The Male Couple: How Relationships Develop* (Englewood Cliffs, N.J.: Prentice-Hall).

[41]Ibid., p. 285. The authors state it this way: "We found that gay men expect mutual emotional dependability with their partners and that relationship fidelity transcends concerns about sexuality and exclusivity."

[42]A. A. Deenen, L. Gijs and A. X. van Naerssen, "Intimacy and Sexuality in Gay Male Couples," *Archives of Sexual Behavior* 23 (1994): 421-31.

[43]As, for example, Robert Williams would urge; see *Just as I Am: A Practical Guide to Being Out, Proud and Christian* (New York: HarperPerennial, 1992).

An emerging area of concern is the move in some pro-gay circles toward acceptance of sexual relations with children before the legal ages of consent. Calls for greater societal acceptance of sexual interactions between adults and the young have not been uncommon in popular and even scholarly venues for discussion of homosexuality. For example, one author urged over a decade ago that such value-loaded terms as "pedophilia" and "child sexual assault" be replaced by the more neutral term "intergenerational intimacy."[44] Concern about this issue reignited recently in response to a sophisticated research article[45] published in an APA journal that urged the same change to "neutral" terminology to describe freely chosen, nonharmful sex between adults and children. The article was applauded by pedophilic organizations, such as the North American Man-Boy Love Association (NAMBLA). Following their meta-analysis of 59 studies of child sexual abuse victims (using college samples), the researchers reasoned that because not all child sexual abuse victims experienced the same extent of harm (and in some cases no harm was recalled) at the time of the abuse and at the time of the various studies, and because some reported the experiences to be pleasurable, that the name "child sexual abuse" should be changed to "adult-child sex." In an attempt to separate morality, societal disapproval and science the researchers argued that "adult-child sex" is a "value neutral term" to be used in cases where there is a "willing encounter with positive reactions."[46] Likewise, "adult-adolescent sex" would be the preferred term for those sexual behaviors that adolescents want and do not report to be harmful. The issue here is that of how the seemingly greater openness of the gay community toward such "intergenerational intimacy" influences our assessment of the relative adaptiveness or maladaptiveness of homosexuality. For traditional Christians who have regarded heterosexual marriage as the only appropriate venue for full sexual intimacy, this openness may be of some concern.

---

[44]Gerald P. Jones, "The Study of Intergenerational Intimacy in North America: Beyond Politics and Pedophilia," *Journal of Homosexuality* 20 (1990): 275-95.

[45]Bruce Rind, Philip Romovitch and Robert Bauserman, "A Meta-Analytic Examination of Assumed properties of Child Sexual Abuse Using College Samples," *Psychological Bulletin* 124 (1998): 22-53.

[46]Ibid., p. 46.

Violation of Societal Norms

Annual studies of public opinion have shown that for over two decades, up to the 1990s, almost 80% of the general public continued to view all instances of homosexual behavior as immoral.[47] This has been true even while support for equal civil rights for homosexuals grew. The majority of Americans are exclusively heterosexual, and there is unquestionably a social stigma attached to being homosexual within a predominantly heterosexual culture. That stigma is, however, slowly eroding; the percentage of Americans each year who report that homosexual behavior is immoral steadily, if slowly, declines.

Interestingly, the mental health community, rather than reflecting the majority view (in the case of homosexuality), seems to have committed itself to revising the predominant public response, to normalizing behavior that is rejected by the public. There is also an effort to do the same thing worldwide, as efforts are in place to change the opinions of numerous psychiatrists around the globe, the majority of whom continue to view same-sex behavior as signaling a pathology.

Conclusion on Scientific Findings

Homosexuality is not officially considered a pathological condition by psychiatry, psychology and other mental health professional organizations. However, determining whether or not homosexuality is inherently pathological is a much more difficult challenge than merely seeing if it is listed in the official manual for diagnosing mental disorders.

We have generated a mixed "scorecard" as we have reviewed evidence related to the four criteria for pathology. Regarding prevalence, we have seen that homosexuality is infrequent compared to heterosexuality. However, without an absolute cutoff point, this finding is not decisive.

The scientific evidence points to a correlation of homosexuality with personal distress, though not all homosexuals are distressed. Many pro-gay advocates view homosexuals who are distressed as the victims of societal prejudice rather than of anything inherently unstable about being gay or lesbian. But it might be instead that the homosexual condition is discordant, or out of alignment, with God's creational intent for

---

[47]Andrew Greeley, R. Michael and T. Smith, "Americans and their Sexual Partners," *Society* 27 (1990): 36-42; Lauman et al., *Social Organization*.

human life and hence unlikely to foster the kind of sense of well-being that goes along with living a fulfilling life.

The arguments regarding maladaptiveness are also inconclusive. Perhaps the greatest concern here is the varying standards by which we might judge maladaptiveness. Although it may be hard to establish a clear definition of maladaptiveness that would be widely accepted in the secular community, certainly Christians must be concerned about relational stability among male homosexuals.

Finally, it is clear that homosexuality violates societal norms, though consensus on these societal norms in America is decaying.

This is a mixed scorecard, reflecting the confusion and disagreement among mental health professionals about the pathological status of homosexuality.

Formal Relevance to the Moral Debate

It does seem comforting to be able to share a common understanding with our broader culture of what is good and bad human behavior, healthy and unhealthy patterns of living. However, we appear to be heading into a time of decreased cultural consensus on a vision of the healthy person. Still, societal judgments of a behavior pattern as unhealthy, disturbed or abnormal remain a vital part of the designation of such a pattern as psychopathological: "Psychopathology is defined by reference to normative patterns of development in normative environmental contexts."[48]

Christians must recognize that neither societal consensus itself, nor societal judgment of a pattern as unhealthy, disturbed or abnormal bears any necessary relation to moral judgment in the Christian tradition. The Old Testament Hebrews were often in the substantial minority in asserting and living by their moral, civil and ceremonial codes. New Testament Christians were certainly out of step with Jewish and Roman understandings of what constituted the "good character," the "good person" and the "good life." Morality is not usually conceived as determined by democratic vote in the Christian tradition.

Also, we are reminded that ethical abnormality and psychological

---

[48]A. Masten and L. Braswell, "Developmental Psychopathology: An Integrative Framework," in *Handbook of Behavior Therapy and Psychological Science*, ed. P. Martin (New York: Pergamon), pp. 35-56.

abnormality are not the same thing, nor are they related *by necessity.* There is no necessary overlap between sinfulness and status as a psychopathology. Many conditions that are "sins" are not pathologies (idolatry, pride, sorcery, lust, fornication). Many conditions that are pathologies are not in themselves sins (anxiety, depression, psychosis). And so it would appear that the removal of homosexuality from the DSM has little clear importance for the moral reasonings of the church as it grapples with the subject of homosexuality.

Homosexuality, as a condition of enduring sexual preference for persons of the same sex, is not the same as homosexual behavior, and it is not subject to the same moral evaluation. The person who experiences same-sex attraction might see these experiences as "a kind of symptomatic participation in the fate of the fallen world," on the same level as our other inclinations or desires to act in defiance to God's plan for his creation.[49] In this sense, homosexuality may not be pathology as mental health professionals understand pathology. However, the experience of same-sex attraction and the identification as gay or lesbian does not appear to be what God wants for people, and this makes further understanding and accurate understanding of homosexuality important for Christians.

Finally, we have seen that there has never been any definitive judgment by the fields of psychiatry or psychology that homosexuality is a healthy lifestyle. But what if it were? Such a judgment would have little bearing on the judgments of the Christian church. In the days of Nero it was healthy and adaptive to worship the Roman emperor. By contemporary American standards a life consumed with greed, materialism, sensualism, selfishness, divorce and pride is judged healthy, but God weighs such a life and finds it lacking.

Summary

☐ Homosexuality is not formally recognized as a mental disorder in the DSM. However, some mental health professionals disagree: a few years following the removal of homosexuality from the DSM, the majority of psychiatrists in America viewed homosexuality as a pathology, and the majority of psychiatrists around the world continue to see same-sex

---

[49]Helmut Thielicke, *The Ethics of Sex,* trans. John W. Doberstein (New York: Harper & Row, 1964), p. 282.

attraction as signaling a mental illness.

☐ Research has shown that it is not the case that *all* homosexuals are *inherently* pathological. Sometimes these findings are misrepresented to suggest that homosexuals do not experience any greater distress than heterosexuals.

☐ Research supports a relationship between homosexuality and personal distress (e.g., rates of depression, substance abuse and suicidality), though not all homosexuals are distressed. Some view the distress as indicating something inherently wrong with homosexuality; others view homosexuals who are distressed as a reflection of societal prejudice.

☐ Research on maladaptiveness is inconclusive primarily because of the lack of agreement as to what constitutes maladaptiveness. The clear evidence of relational instability and promiscuity among male homosexuals must figure as problematic for Christians.

☐ Homosexuality violates societal norms; however, mental health organizations have taken the formal position that societal norms have to be changed toward accepting homosexuality as a normal sexual variant.

☐ Research on whether homosexuality is a pathological condition is not formally relevant to the moral debate in the church. Psychological abnormality and immorality are two different things, although sometimes they overlap.

Discussion Questions

1. What do you think about the apparent lack of protocol in the decision to remove homosexuality from the DSM?

2. How important is it to have a *representative* sample of homosexuals when making claims about the homosexual population?

3. Do you think higher rates of depression, substance abuse and suicidality among homosexuals is a symptom of the maladaptivess of a homosexual orientation, the result of societal prejudice and oppression, or some combination?

4. How relevant is the question of whether homosexuality is a psychopathology to the moral debate in the church?

5

Can Homosexuality
Be Changed?

But why ought we to obey instincts? Is there another instinct of a higher order directing us to do so, and a third of a still higher order directing us to obey *it*? —an infinite
regress of instincts? This is presumably impossible, but nothing else will serve. From
the statement of psychological fact "I have an impulse to do so and so" we cannot by
any ingenuity derive the practical principle "I ought to obey this impulse." ...
    Telling us to obey instinct is like telling us to obey "people." People say different
things: so do instincts. Our instincts are at war.
— C. S. LEWIS, *THE ABOLITION OF MAN*

S *everal groups —including the Christian Coalition, Family First and the*
Family Research Council—recently sponsored full-page newspaper ads in several major national newspapers. Some of the
ads promoted ex-gay ministries, claiming that "thousands are
leaving their homosexual identity for sexual celibacy, and even marriage."

Ads were then run in response to the "ex-gay" ads. These ads featured
gay and lesbian young adults and their parents. The message was that
homosexuality is not a condition a person can or should change. Homosexuality is an identity to embrace.

This exchange of full-page advertisements in prominent newspapers
has contributed to a national discussion about whether or not homosexuality can be changed. The church has certainly been affected by this
debate, and many church documents studying human sexuality and, in
particular, homosexuality are claiming that science has something relevant to say to the moral debate.

Use of Research in Church Debates on Whether Homosexuality Can Be Changed

Chandler Burr, in a chapter in a book promoting church dialogue on homosexuality (which was previously published as an article in *Atlantic Monthly*), makes a strong claim about whether homosexuality can be changed. He claims that "five decades of psychiatric evidence demonstrates that homosexuality is immutable."[1] The word *immutable* means "unchangeable" or "impossible to change." This is a strong and direct claim. According to Burr, scientific research has clearly shown that homosexuality cannot be changed.

A similar claim is made in a booklet promoting church dialogue on gay and lesbian issues. Using a questionnaire on homosexuality adapted from a Dear Abby column entitled "True-False Quiz on Homosexuality Is Worth Repeating—and Retaining," Thorson-Smith says the correct answer is "false" to the question, "With proper therapy and motivation, a [lesbian or gay man] can become [heterosexual]."[2] Science is presumed to tell the informed reader that homosexuality cannot be changed. Such arguments occur often throughout the sexuality literature of the late twentieth-century church.

Finally, let us return again to the arguments of Myers.[3] He states boldly that "efforts to change one's sexual orientation usually (some say, virtually always) fail."[4] He cites two kinds of "evidence" here. First, he approvingly quotes Haldeman's claim (discussed below) that there is no evidence that homosexual orientation can be changed. The simple problem here is that this is a fallacious claim; the evidence may be debatable or unconvincing to some, but that is not the same as saying that there is no evidence. Second, Myers cites a string of anecdotes about people who tried to change and failed to do so, including a number of prominent former leaders in the change movement. The major

---

[1] Chandler Burr, "Homosexuality and Biology," in *Homosexuality in the Church: Both Sides of the Debate*, ed. Jeffrey S. Siker (Louisville, Ky.: Westminster John Knox, 1993), p. 65.

[2] From Sylvia Thorson-Smith, *Reconciling the Broken Silence: The Church in Dialogue on Gay and Lesbian Issues* (Louisville, Ky.: Christian Education Program Area of the Congregational Ministry Division, Presbyterian Church USA), p. 42.

[3] David G. Myers, "A Levels-of-Explanation View," in *Psychology and Christianity: Four Views*, ed. Eric L. Johnson and Stanton L. Jones (Downers Grove, Ill.: InterVarsity Press, 2000), pp. 54-83.

[4] Ibid., p. 78.

problem with such an argument is that you cannot cite one type of anecdotal evidence (failures to change) and totally dismiss the opposite types of anecdotes (change success stories); Myers fails to consider even one anecdotal story of success. In short, Myers's dismissal of all evidence that change occurs does not appear to treat fairly either type of evidence, scientific or anecdotal.

But what difference does this claim make? This claim, as best we can tell, tends to be put to three different uses in the hands of those urging the Christian church to change its moral stance.

First, if it can be shown that homosexual orientation is immutable, then that finding challenges either the truthfulness of Scripture or our interpretations of it. Conservative Christians often quote the words of the apostle Paul, who stated:

> Do you not know that the wicked will not inherit the kingdom of God? Do not be deceived: Neither the sexually immoral nor idolaters nor adulterers nor male prostitutes nor homosexual offenders nor thieves nor the greedy nor drunkards nor slanderers nor swindlers will inherit the kingdom of God. And that is what some of you were. But you were washed, you were sanctified, you were justified in the name of the Lord Jesus Christ and by the Spirit of our God. (1 Cor 6:9-11)

If homosexual orientation cannot change, then Paul is either wrong in claiming "that is what some of you were" or he meant something different than change of orientation.

Second, and returning to a theme touched on at the end of the previous chapter, proof that homosexuals cannot change may paint the traditionalist position as heartless. After all, if homosexuals cannot change their orientation, then they are consigned to permanent chastity, and that not because they choose to remain single but because singleness is their only option because of their sexual orientation.

Third, proof that homosexuals cannot change can function as an indirect attack against the traditional position. How? Again the notion of knocking down a caricature of the traditional position comes up. Traditionalists are portrayed as claiming that all homosexuals can change if they really wanted to. For example, the discussion guide we cited in previous chapters portrays traditionalists as believing that "the orientation of all homosexual persons can be modified to conform to the heterosexual norm through conversion and healing."[5] It is supposed that if conversion to heterosexuality can be shown to be impossible, the traditionalist case is considerably weakened. To the degree that this is truly a core assertion of the traditionalists,[6] the effectiveness of "conversion" therapies becomes relevant to the moral debate. If the behavioral sciences can show that sexual orientation is in fact immutable, or that change is at least tremendously difficult for the majority, then the traditionalist position appears untenable.

One final point before we engage the scientific research and find out what it actually tells us. The discussion on this point tends to get bogged down in logically clean but unworkable categories. To claim that "homosexual orientation is immutable" is to make a universal claim: there has never and will never be any instance whatsoever of a person changing a homosexual orientation. Framed in this language, even one case in all of history would falsify this universal claim; one healed homosexual makes it *not true* that homosexuals cannot change. The same point works in the other direction: if a traditionalist claims that every homosexual can change, then it only takes one case of a person who cannot change to falsify the universal claim. In the battle between the exclusive universal claims, no one has the advantage. When traditionalists claim examples of change, the gay community can claim that the research was fraudulent, that the person was not a true homosexual[7] or some such claim. When "progressives" claim examples of people who failed to change, the conservative Christian community can claim that the person who tried to change was not really sincere or had secret sin in his or her life that blocked God's work of healing or some such explanation.

---

[5]Province VII's Committee on the Study of Human Sexuality, *Human Sexuality: A Christian Perspective: A Study Course and Leader's Guide Prepared for Province VII* (Lubbock, Tex.: Province VII [Diocese of Northwest Texas], 1992), p. 63.

[6]But remember what the newspaper ads cited earlier actually said: "Thousands are leaving their homosexual identity for sexual celibacy, and even marriage." The ads did not say, "Thousands, indeed all who try, are being healed from their homosexual identity and enabled to enter a fulfilling marriage." Even Paul says (in paraphrase), "some of you were homosexual offenders," a statement that leaves it unclear whether Paul means that they became heterosexuals or simply ceased offending in a homosexual manner (i.e., engaging in homosexual behavior).

[7]This claim is an interesting one that insulates the statement "homosexuality is immutable" from ever being refuted; all instances of change can be dismissed as involving false homosexuals. Of course, in science, claims that are never falsifiable are usually treated as meaningless.

There are two key points in getting out of the box constructed by these two universal claims: (1) Note that it is not necessary to formulate our options just in terms of these two universal claims: the third alternative is, simply, that "some homosexuals can change." (2) Note that we must be clear about what we mean by change. In particular, we must ask if the person who leaves the "gay lifestyle" and becomes a well-adjusted celibate single person (but never "becomes a heterosexual") is healed.

Research on Whether Homosexuality Can Be Changed

However the orientation toward homosexual preference develops, there is substantial agreement that it is not a preference that can be easily changed by a simple act of the will. Methods of change have included psychoanalysis and other depth psychology approaches, behavioral therapy, aversion therapy, Adlerian therapy and group therapies offered from psychoanalytic, experiential and social learning perspectives.

Most of the published empirical studies on change were conducted during the 1950s, 1960s and 1970s (although there are many counselors and analysts who apparently continue to provide treatment to change sexual orientation, as we shall discuss below). The early research on change was often of poor methodological quality by today's standards. Methodology refers to the way the study was designed, the measures of change, definitions of success and so on. Measures of change in the older research, for example, were often based on the judgements of the persons serving as therapists, and often these ratings used categories (such as Very Improved and Somewhat Improved) that fail to provide detailed information about change. When the patients themselves were queried, their self-reports were again quite simplistic, ranging from patients reporting that they changed their orientation, to patients reporting that they reduced or discontinued homosexual contacts, to patients reporting, that they successfully engaged in heterosexual sex. Use of therapists' ratings is particular problematic by today's standards, based on concern that the therapists have a vested interested in reporting their own success. Rigorous examinations of indices of sexual orientation were rarely if ever used. At the other extreme, only a few studies used physiological measures of change, such as measures of sexual arousal to various visual stimuli. The studies that used the latter types of measures of change often attempted to change sexual behavior and reduce anxiety about heterosexual sex.

Individual treatment. Numerous reports have been published on change of homosexual behavior or orientation. A simple summary of the most important individual therapy studies is presented in table 5.1. Several of these are important enough to discuss in greater detail.

1. Psychoanalytic and psychodynamic interventions. Houston MacIntosh[8] published data based on a recent, semirandom survey of psychoanalysts (which had an unusually high response rate of 67.5%). Among respondents 274 analysts reported working with 1,215 homosexual patients. Of the homosexual patients treated, analysts reported that 276 (22.7% with 23.9% of males and 20.2% of females) changed their sexual orientation from homosexual to heterosexual, and 84.0% obtained "significant therapeutic benefit" (again, the sexes were nearly identical, with 85.3% of males and 81.3% of females achieving "significant therapeutic benefit").[9] Both male and female patients spent an average of about four years in analysis.

An additional interesting finding was that the vast majority of analysts surveyed (97.6%) did *not* agree with the statement that a "homosexual patient 'can and should' change to heterosexuality." This flies in the face of charges that analysts are prejudiced by society's negative view of homosexuality or that analysts are unable to muster the neutrality needed to provide analysis. (In fact, MacIntosh shares that these very assertions by Richard Isay, the chair of the American Psychiatric Association's Committee on Gay, Lesbian, and Bisexual Issues, are what motivated him to conduct the survey.) Moreover, although most analysts (62.3%) reported believing that homosexual patients "sometimes" change their sexual orientation, only 4.2% reported believing that change of orientation happens "frequently."[10]

In a follow-up report MacIntosh[11] examined some of the factors related

---

[8]Houston MacIntosh, "Attitudes and Experiences of Psychoanalysts," *Journal of the American Psychoanalytic Association* 42, no. 4 (1994): 1183-1207.

[9]Ibid., p. 1189. According to MacIntosh, post hoc analyses suggest that the change rate for male homosexuals is not significantly different (two-tail t-test, $p = .45$) from the 27% change rate reported by Irving Bieber and his colleagues over 35 years ago in *Homosexuality: A Psychoanalytic Study* (New York: Basic Books, 1962).

[10]Ibid., p. 1188 (table 2).

[11]Houston MacIntosh, "Factors Associated with Outcome of Psychoanalysis of Homosexual Patients," *British Journal of Psychotherapy* 13 (1997): 358-68.

Study	Theoretical orientation	N	O	IP	NC	UC	%PO
*†Bieber et al. (1962)	Psychoanalytic	106	29	4	58	15	27
Cantom-Dutari (1974)	Behavioral	49	19				39
*Freeman & Meyer (1975)	Behavioral	11	9		2		82
*Hadfield (1958)	Psychoanalytic	9	6			3	67
*Hatterer (1970)	Psychoanalytic	143	49	18	76		34
*†‡Kaye et al. (1967)	Psychoanalytic	24	6			18	25
McConaghy (1970)	Aversion	40	10				25
*†MacIntosh (1994)	Psychoanalysis	1215	276				23
*MacCulloch & Feldman (1967)	Aversion	35	10				29
*Masters & Johnson (1979)	Behavioral	67	29				43
Mayerson & Lief (1965)	Unspecified	19	9		10		47
Schwartz & Masters (1984)	Behavioral	54	35				65
*Socarides (1978)	Psychoanalytic	45	20			25	44
*van den Aardweg (1986)	Adlerian	101	37	11	9	43	37

Table 5.1. Individual treatments for homosexuality (1950s-1990s). Irving Bieber et al., *Homosexuality: A Psychoanalytic Study* (New York: Basic Books, 1962); Alejandro Cantom-Dutari, "Combined Intervention for Controlling Unwanted Homosexual Behavior," *Archives of Sexual Behavior* 3 (1974): 367-25; William Freeman and Robert G. Meyer, "A Behavioral Alteration of Sexual Preferences in the Human Male," *Behavior Therapy* 6 (1975): 206-12; J. A. Hadfield, "The Cure of Homosexuality," *British Medical Journal,* June 7, 1958, pp. 1323-26; Lawrence Hatterer, *Changing Heterosexuality in the Male: Treatment for Men Troubled by Homosexuality* (New York: McGraw-Hill, 1970); Harvey E. Kaye et al., "Homosexuality in Women," *Archives of General Psychiatry* 17 (1967): 626-34; Nathaniel McConaghy, "Subjective and Penile Plethysmograph Responses to Aversion Therapy for Homosexuality: A Follow-Up Study," *British Journal of Psychiatry* 117 (1970): 555-60; Houston MacIntosh, "Attitudes and Experiences of Psychoanalysts," *Journal of the American Psychoanalytic Association* 42, no. 4 (1994): 1183-207; M. J. MacCulloch and M. P. Feldman, "Aversion Therapy in Management of 43 Homosexuals," *British Medical Journal* 2 (1967): 594-97; William H. Masters and Virginia E. Johnson, *Homosexuality in Perspective* (Boston: Little, Brown, 1979); Peter Mayerson and Harold I. Lief, "Psychotherapy of Homosexuals: A Follow-Up Study of Nineteen Cases" in *Sexual Inversion: The Multiple Roots of Homosexuality,* ed. Judd Marmor (New York: Basic Books, 1965), pp. 302-44; Mark F. Schwartz and William H. Masters, "The Masters and Johnson Treatment Program for Dissatisfied Homosexual Men," *American Journal of Psychiatry* 141 (1984): 173-81; Charles W. Socarides, *Homosexuality* (New York: Jason Aronson, 1978); Gerard van den Aardweg, *On the Origins and Treatment of Homosexuality* (Westport, Conn.: Praeger, 1985).

N = total number of patients in study. PO = Positive Outcome. IP = In Progress. NC = No change. UC = Unclear. %PO = Percentage with Positive Outcome ($\bar{x} = 41.92\%$). *See Goetze for a detailed review of methodology, definition of change, and summary of results with special emphasis on change from exclusively homosexual to exclusively heterosexual. ‡Study of females exclusively. †Figures based on psychoanalysts' responses to survey questionnaire.

to change of sexual orientation in his previous survey. Factors associated with change of orientation included analysts' expectation of change (positive expectancy was related to greater likelihood to report change). Factors associated with significant therapeutic benefit were length of treatment (especially for males), change of sexual oriention (less so for females), and gender of analyst. ("Female analysts report a significantly higher rate of significant therapeutic benefit for their female patients than male analysts report for their female patients"[12]) The gender of the analyst is complicated by length of treatment, as female analysts reported seeing female patients longer than did male analysts.

Before we move on from the MacIntosh study, we want to highlight the limitations inherent in this type of survey. Robert Goetze[13] identifies several limitations to this type of therapist survey research, including the possibility that psychoanalysts misapplied the labels "homosexual" and "heterosexual." It is conceivable that some of the analysts mislabeled bisexuals as homosexuals and then mistook heterosexual adaptation by the bisexuals as true heterosexuality. Also, the reports of the psychoanalysts were not corroborated by reports from patients themselves or other objective measures of sexual identity or behavior. The standard practice in the evaluation of psychotherapy is not to rely on therapist report of change but rather to primarily study patient experience directly; this study is quite deficient by this standard.

Although the survey by MacIntosh is the largest study published in recent years, it is certainly not the only study. The remaining data are from much smaller, and mostly older, studies (with one major exception—the NARTH study discussed later). Most of the studies, further, were done only with male homosexuals. The studies that were done from the perspective of psychodynamic therapy[14] are almost all outcome reports from the therapists, which are, as we have noted, of limited value

---

[12]Ibid., p. 365.

[13]Robert M. Goetze, *Homosexuality and the Possibility of Change: A Review of 17 Published Studies* (New Direction for Life of Canada), <www.newdirection.ca/a_chang2.htm>.

[14]Psychodynamic therapies are those that tend to focus on "depth change"; they tend to focus less on resolving discrete problems and more on the (hypothesized) underlying psychological conditions that cause the problems. Another characteristic of psychodynamic therapy is the intent to use the intense relationship that develops between patient and therapist as the "test tube" or relational crucible in which the patient's difficulties get worked out. Examples of such psychodynamic therapies include psychoanalysis, psycho-

by today's standards for topnotch psychotherapy research. For example, Lawrence Hatterer[15] reports on his work with 143 homosexual men. Of the 143 homosexual men in the study, Hatterer reports that 49 changed their sexual orientation to heterosexual, 18 experienced a partial change to heterosexuality, and 76 remained homosexual. Similarly, Gerard van den Aardweg[16] reported on his work with 101 homosexual patients based on a depth psychology approach that draws on psychoanalytic and Adlerian theories ("anticomplaining therapy"). He reports that nearly half (43) of the men he treated dropped out of treatment. Eleven percent of the total 101 patients experienced "radical change" from homosexuality, while 26% experienced "satisfactory change," 11% "improved," and 9% showed "no improvement." These reports of change are based on interviews by van den Aardweg with his patients and were not corroborated by external measures. Again, however, a number of patients reported change of orientation, and these kinds of reports certainly appear to provide a rationale for more research on the effectiveness of change methods.

Not all of the psychoanalytic studies are therapist surveys. An attempt at a more formal outcome evaluation was reported by Hadfield.[17] He published more complete findings on individual psychoanalysis with nine patients. It is unclear what progress was made among three of the nine patients. Relatively clear and positive outcomes were described for the other six patients in treatment. Positive outcomes were defined as adjustment from either exclusive homosexuality to heterosexuality (four patients) or predominant homosexuality to heterosexuality (two patients).

2. Nicolosi's reparative therapy. Although a surprisingly high percentage of professionals report attempting to change clients' sexual orientation (as we will discuss later), very few *publish* any reports of their work or of

---

analytic psychotherapy, Jungian psychotherapy, ego psychology, object relations psychology and perhaps some versions of Adlerian psychotherapy; see Stanton L. Jones and Richard E. Butman, *Modern Psychotherapies: A Comprehensive Christian Appraisal* (Downers Grove, Ill.: InterVarsity Press, 1991).

[15]Lawrence Hatterer, *Changing Heterosexuality in the Male: Treatment for Men Troubled by Homosexuality* (New York: McGraw-Hill, 1970).

[16]Van den Aardweg, *On the Origins*, pp. 195-200.

[17]Hadfield, "Cure of Homosexuality," pp. 1323-26.

the changes produced. One major and very controversial exception to this trend is Joseph Nicolosi,[18] a psychologist in California who has written about reparative therapy of male homosexuals. We will discuss this therapeutic approach briefly to give the reader a better idea of what one therapeutic approach looks like.

Reparative therapy is a form of psychodynamic therapy that attempts to repair the male gender identity in male homosexuals. Repair is needed, Nicolosi argues, because male homosexuals have failed to have their own legitimate developmental needs met in childhood. As a result, they have sexualized other males because they failed to identify with them earlier in life:

> Homosexuality is a developmental problem that is almost always the result of problems in family relations, particularly between father and son. As a result of failure with father, the boy does not fully internalize male gender-identity, and develops homosexuality.[19]

Nicolosi's treatment of male homosexuals consists of both individual and group therapy. Individual therapy provides an intense relationship with the therapist that allows for the eventual working through of developmental needs. Emphasis is placed on self-acceptance, nonsexual intimacy with other males and clarification of perceptions of what it means to possess masculinity. According to Nicolosi, clients typically resolve issues with their fathers (particularly anger), and work toward forgiveness:

> Forgiveness of father is not an easy task because it often means accepting father for who he is, with his limitations, including his limited ability to demonstrate love, affection, and acceptance. It often feels like a death experience for a young man when he realizes that he must bury once and for all the fantasy of receiving his father's love. To understand and forgive and love his father is, paradoxically, to be father to his father—to give him what he, the son, would have desired. Compassion for father is the final step of forgiveness. Often compassion grows out of an understanding of his father's father, and how he treated his own son.[20]

Group therapy also plays an important part in reparative therapy.

---

[18] Joseph Nicolosi, *Reparative Therapy of Male Homosexuality: A New Clinical Approach* (Northvale, N.J.: Jason Aronson, 1991); Joseph Nicolosi, *Healing Homosexuality: Case Stories of Reparative Therapy* (Northvale, N.J.: Jason Aronson, 1993).

[19] Nicolosi, *Reparative Therapy*, p. 25.

[20] Ibid., p. 161.

According to Nicolosi, group therapy provides a setting in which men experience support, encouragement and mutuality. One of the central treatment issues, defensive detachment ("the blocking mechanism that prevents male bonding and identification"[21]), is addressed most dramatically through group therapy interactions. *Defensive detachment* is Nicolosi's term that is used to describe a pattern of hanging back (detachment) in fear (defensiveness is the motivation) from full engagement with a person's interpersonal relationships. The defensively detached individual is seen as using humor, cynicism, intellectualization and other defensive patterns to protect himself from full awareness of himself and his problems. Group therapy becomes an arena in which to break down this pattern. Group therapy also provides a place for clients to work through transference and anger. "Success" in reparative therapy is not seen as a quick gain over the course of a few weeks. Rather, Nicolosi presents it as a lifelong process for some who pursue change:

> The acquisition of masculine identity may be a lifetime process. Yet no matter what a man's earlier deprivations, opportunities remain available throughout life to grow toward wholeness.[22]

3. Psychoanalysis with women. In a rare examination of homosexuality in women, Harvey Kaye and his colleagues[23] surveyed psychoanalysts who worked with female homosexuals and then compared those results to nonhomosexual female patients. Only 24 patients were actually discussed, and data was available on only 19 of these. Of the 24 "homosexual" women studied, six experienced improvement. However, Goetze[24] identifies several limitations to this study, the most significant being that the definition of homosexuality focused on same-sex behavior. There

---

[21]Ibid., p. 211.

[22]Ibid., p. 218. For additional information on reparative therapy, see Elizabeth Moberly's *Homosexuality: A New Christian Ethic* (Cambridge: James Clarke, 1983), where she discusses her perspective on "defensive detachment," which she believes occurs when homosexual persons fail to attach or identify with their same-sex parent. According to Moberly, homosexuality is essentially same-sex relational "ambivalence": "In short, homosexuality is a phenomenon of same-sex ambivalence, not just same-sex love; and it is in itself a relational deficit vis a vis the same sex rather than vis a vis the opposite sex" (p. 17).

[23]Harvey E. Kaye, Soll Berl, Jack Clare, Mary R. Eleston, Benjamin S. Gershwin, Patricia Gershwin, Leonard S. Kogan, Clara Torda and Cornelia B. Wilbur, "Homosexuality in Women," *Archives of General Psychiatry* 17 (1967): 626-34.

[24]Goetze, *Homosexuality and the Possibility*, pp. 28-29.

does appear to be movement from homosexuality (as defined) to heterosexuality; however the limitations to the study suggest that support for
change will likely have to come from other studies.

4. Behavioral interventions.[25] A number of behavioral interventions of
various sorts are reported in table 5.1. We will briefly discuss several.
William Freeman and Robert Meyer[26] reported on the behavioral treatment of 11 homosexual men. All of the 11 men reportedly changed their
experience of same-sex attraction, and 9 were reported to have main-
tained a "heterosexual adjustment" at the eighteenth-month follow-up.
The presence of a follow-up is an important advance in assessment of
therapy outcomes, but the continuing use of global outcome categories
("heterosexual adjustment") is a major problem.

Nathaniel McConaghy[27] discusses some of the research on change
of sexual behavior by behavioral professionals. He contends that sexual orientation cannot be changed but that people can change their sexual behavior, and they can certainly choose how they want to identify
themselves to others. Referring to the clients who pursue behavioral
change, McConaghy states: "Though their basic orientation cannot be
changed, they can determine how they express that orientation and
how they identify to themselves and to others."[28] McConaghy is particularly concerned to leave open the option of individuals of homosexual
orientation seeking to live a satisfying married life. In his own outcome
research McConaghy[29] has utilized penile plethysmograph responses

---

[25] Behavioral interventions tend to be much more "symptom oriented" than the psychodynamic therapies; they are more likely to directly target the elimination of undesired
behavior and the establishment of desired behavior.

[26] William Freeman and Robert G. Meyer, "A Behavioral Alteration of Sexual Preferences
in the Human Male," *Behavior Therapy* 6 (1975): 206-12.

[27] Nathaniel McConaghy, "Sexual Deviation," in *International Handbook of Behavior Modifica-
tion and Therapy,* ed. Alan S. Bellack, Michael Hersen and Alan E. Kazdin, 2nd ed. (New
York: Plenum, 1990), pp. 565-80; Nathaniel McConaghy, *Sexual Behavior* (New York:
Plenum, 1993).

[28] Nathaniel McConaghy, "Sexual Deviation," p. 577.

[29] Nathaniel McConaghy, "Subjective and Penile Plethysmograph Responses Following
Aversion-Relief and Apomorphine Aversion Therapy for Homosexual Impulses," *British
Journal of Psychiatry* 115 (1969): 723-30; Nathaniel McConaghy, "Subjective and Penile
Plethysmograph Responses to Aversion Therapy for Homosexuality: A Follow-up," *Brit-
ish Journal of Psychiatry* 117 (1970): 555-60; Nathaniel McConaghy, "Is a Homosexual
Orientation Irreversible?" *British Journal of Psychiatry* 129 (1976): 556-63.

that measure the amount of arousal a man experiences to various visual images by recording subtle physiological changes in the man's penis. Utilizing behavioral and aversion therapy techniques, he has helped people manage impulses, feelings and behaviors that they otherwise experienced as compulsive. He reports successfully reduced anxiety among homosexuals who were interested in pursuing heterosexual behaviors or relationships.

5. Abstinence approach. In addition to the behavior-focused interventions discussed above, Michael Lundy and George Rekers[30] review other approaches to homosexual persons, particularly adolescents. From their perspective, abstinence-based programs are a promising approach to alter destructive patterns that might be set up by early sexual debut, including same-sex behavior. The authors encourage intervention to change high-risk sexual behaviors that can lead to sexually transmitted diseases (STDs) and the spread of AIDS through abstinence. In contrast to McConaghy, Lundy and Rekers do discuss interventions to modify sexual orientation and underscore the importance of high motivation for change (including family/environmental support) and relatively little previous same-sex behavior. Lundy and Rekers observe that "basic behavioral techniques used to alter pathological sexual behavior"[31] can be used to help change behaviors and sexual orientation. The authors also discuss the often-overlooked issues related to providing therapy to adolescents who contend with same-sex attraction, including the importance of addressing family dynamics that provide a supportive environment for change.

6. Group treatments. Mental health professionals have also provided group treatment to homosexuals who have pursued change of sexual orientation or behavior. Sometimes people were seen in individual treatment either prior to or concomitant with group therapy. In any case, Rogers, Roback, McKee and Calhoun[32] reviewed both inpatient

---

[30]Michael S. Lundy and George A. Rekers, "Homosexuality in Adolescence: Interventions and Ethical Considerations," in *Handbook of Child and Adolescent Sexual Problems* (New York: Lexington Books, 1995), pp. 348-52.

[31]Ibid., p. 364.

[32]Carl Rogers, Howard Roback, Embry McKee, and Daniel Calhoun, "Group Psychotherapy with Homosexuals: A Review," *International Journal of Group Psychotherapy* 26 (1976): 3-27.

and outpatient group therapies for homosexuals published during the 1950s-1970s. In a recent review of their findings, we discussed the percentage of positive outcomes from the outpatient studies.[33] The findings from these reports of group therapies are summarized in table 5.2.

We will highlight a few of these studies, as we did with the individual treatment approaches mentioned above. Let us consider the two outcome studies that used control groups to make comparisons. The use of control groups represents a major improvement in the level of sophistication of the study outcomes. In one of the more detailed studies published during the 1970s, the researchers reported[34] on 30 male homosexuals (20 who received treatment and 10 who made up the control group). On measures of homosexual thoughts and fantasy, the 20 homosexuals who were in treatment improved significantly when compared to the control group. Similar findings were reported on measures of frequency of homosexual preoccupation (although the control group was less preoccupied at the outset, which complicates our understanding of this finding).

The authors later published a study[35] of 50 homosexual males (30 in treatment and 20 in the control group). Twenty-five of the 30 homosexuals in the treatment group completed treatment, and positive outcomes as compared to the control group were reported on measures of persistence of homosexual fantasy and preoccupation, as well as sexual behavior, including dating and heterosexual intercourse (although the control group also experienced some improvement). These are encouraging findings (for those who believe or want to believe in the possibility of change), but it is worth noting that reports of "significant changes" or "positive movement" beg the question of whether the magnitude of the change brought about in the life of the patient achieved "clinical significance," that is, was sufficient to "put the patient on a new path in life." By analogy, an innovative approach to marital therapy might reduce marital fights by 40% (a good outcome), but if it does

---

[33]Mark A. Yarhouse, "Group Therapies for Homosexual Seeking Change," *Journal of Psychology and Theology* 26, no. 3 (1998): 247-58.

[34]Richard A. Truax, William S. Moeller and Garfield Tourney, "The Medical Approach to Male Homosexuality," *Journal of the Iowa Medical Society* 60 (1970): 397-403.

[35]Richard A. Truax and Garfield Tourney, "Male Homosexuals in Group Psychotherapy," *Diseases of the Nervous System* 32 (1971): 707-11.

Study	Theoretical orientation	N	PO	IP	NC	UN	%PO
Eliasberg (1954)	psychoanalytic	6	3	1	1	1	50%
Hadden (1958)	psychoanalytic	3	1	2			33%
Hadden (1966)	psychoanalytic	32	12	20			38%
Singer & Fischer (1967)	psychoanalytic	8	4				50%
Litman (1961)	psychoanalytic	1		1			
*Truax et al. (1970)	psychoanalytic	20		20			
*Truax & Tourney (1971)	psychoanalytic	30	20	5	5		67%
Birk (1974)	social learning	66	14	15			21%
Beukenkamp (1960)	experiential	1	1				100%
Mintz (1966)	unknown	10	3	3	1	3	30%
Johnsgard & Schumacher (1970)	unknown	5			5		
Stone et al. (1966)	unknown	1		1			
Pittman & DeYoung (1971)	unknown	6	3	1	2		50%
Munzer (1965)	unknown	18	5	2	1	10	28%
Finney (1960)	unknown	3	2			1	67%
Covi (1972)	unknown	30		8			

Table 5.2. Group treatments for homosexuality (1950s-1970s). W. G. Eliasberg, "Group Treatments of Homosexuals on Probation," *Group Psychotherapy* 7 (1954): 218-26; Samuel B. Hadden, "Treatment of Homosexuality in Individual and Group Psychotherapy," *American Journal of Psychiatry* 114 (1958): 810-15; Samuel B. Hadden, "Treatment of Male Homosexuals in Groups," *International Journal of Group Psychotherapy* 16 (1966): 13-22; Melvin Singer and Ruth Fischer, "Group Psychotherapy of Male Homosexuals by a Male and Female Co-Therapy Team," *International Journal of Group Psychotherapy* 17 (1967): 44-52; Robert E. Litman, "Psychotherapy of a Homosexual Man in a Heterosexual Group," *International Journal of Group Psychotherapy* 11 (1961): 440-48; Richard A. Truax, William S. Moeller and Garfield Tourney, "The Medical Approach to Male Homosexuality," *Journal of the Iowa Medical Society* 60 (1970): 397-403; Richard A. Truax and Garfield Tourney, "Male Homosexuals in Group Psychotherapy," *Diseases of the Nervous System* 32 (1971): 707-11; Lee Birk, "Group Psychotherapy for Men Who Are Homosexual," *Journal of Sex and Marital Therapy* 1 (1974): 29-52; C. Beukenkamp, "Phantom Patricide," *Archives of General Psychiatry* 3 (1960): 282-88; Elizabeth E. Mintz, "Overt Male Homosexuals in Combined Group and Individual Treatment," *Journal of Consulting Psychology* 30 (1966): 193-98; Keith W. Johnsgard and Ray M. Schumacher, "The Experience of Intimacy in Group Psychotherapy with Male Homosexuals," *Psychotherapy: Theory, Research, and Practice* 7 (1970): 173-76; Walter N. Stone, John Schengber and F. Stanley Seifried, "The Treatment of a Homosexual Woman in a Mixed Group," *International Journal of Group Psychotherapy* 16 (1966): 425-32; Frank S. Pittman and Carol D. DeYoung, "The Treatment of Homosexuals in Heterogeneous Groups," *International Journal of Group Psychotherapy* 21 (1971): 62-73; J. Munzer, "Treatment of the Homosexual in Group Psychotherapy," *Topical Problems of Psychotherapy* 5 (1965): 164-69; Joseph C. Finney, "Homosexuality Treated by Combined Therapy," *Journal of the Society of Therapists* 6 (1960): 27-34; L. Covi, "A Group Psychotherapy Approach to the Treatment of Neurotic Symptoms in Male and Female Patients of Homosexual Preference," *Psychotherapy and Psychosomatics* 20 (1972): 176-80.

N = total number of clients in study. PO = Positive Outcome. IP = In Progress. NC = No Change. UN = Unknown. %PO = Percentage with positive outcome as measured by therapist or self-report ($\bar{x}$ = 33.4%). *Utilized a control group. Reproduced with permission from *Journal of Psychology and Theology* 26, no. 3 (1998).

not produce more happiness and commitment in the marriage, and if two years later the divorce rate is the same, then the change that was brought about failed to achieve true clinical significance.

The other group therapy studies did not use control groups. However, the findings may still be important, as those who struggle with experiences of same-sex attraction and pursue change will still want to know what these groups have to offer. Groups have been offered from psychoanalytic, experiential and social learning perspectives, and positive outcomes were reported in the majority of published reports. For example, Samuel Hadden[36] reported on 32 male homosexuals in group treatment. Twelve of the 32 reportedly changed sexual orientation. Again, some studies emphasize a "heterosexual adjustment" while others emphasize increased heterosexual behavior and fantasy or decreased preoccupation with homosexual fantasy. Frank Pittman and Carol DeYoung,[37] for example, reported on a total of 30 patients (not all of whom were exclusively homosexual to begin with). But of the six homosexual men in group treatment, three "chose to change and to give up homosexual contacts."[38]

There does appear to be evidence that some level of change can be expected by a percentage of people who pursue treatment. That change may be at a behavioral level, or it may be a change in fantasies or thought life, including preoccupation with unwanted thoughts. Or it is possible that it is change of sexual orientation, if therapist and self-report are any indication and can be trusted. Again, there are many limitations to these studies. Most did not use a control group to see what kind of progress patients would make if they were not in treatment. Also, as we mentioned above, there is little consistency across studies as to what constitutes "positive outcome." Definitions included decreased homosexual contact, reported desire to increase heterosexual contact, reported desire for heterosexual marriage, therapist report of change, and patient self-report of change of sexual orientation.

We can certainly lament the lack of sophisticated methodology in

---

[36]Samuel B. Hadden, "Treatment of Male Homosexuals in Groups," *International Journal of Group Psychotherapy* 16 (1966): 13-22.

[37]Frank S. Pittman and Carol D. DeYoung, "The Treatment of Homosexuals in Heterogeneous Groups," *International Journal of Group Psychotherapy* 21 (1971): 62-73.

[38]Ibid., p. 66.

these studies. And they cannot be cited as incontrovertible evidence that homosexual orientation can change to heterosexual orientation. However, some people who pursue change of behavior, thoughts or orientation will be encouraged to see evidence that change of same-sex behavior and impulses and perhaps orientation occurred for a percentage of people in treatment. The average positive outcome across these studies is about 33%. While this is surely not a stunningly high rate of success, it is certainly not out of line with the reported success rates for dealing with the more difficult and stable psychological disorders like the personality disorders or the addictions. So we can say that "in light of the indication that some change of impulses and behavior (and perhaps orientation) occurs in group therapy, it would be a mistake to dismiss this research as having nothing of relevance to say to those who seek change."[39] We are reminded that the lack of sophisticated methodology does not disprove the success of these treatments; rather, it challenges researchers to provide more sophisticated program evaluations and outcome studies to further clarify what clients can expect from various programs.

Christian Support Groups and "Healing" Ministries

We mentioned at the outset of this chapter that recent ads in national newspapers claiming change of sexual orientation have brought a significant amount of attention to those religiously based groups that provide support to homosexuals seeking change. It should be noted that many Christian support ministries work with a range of sexual issues, some of which are related to homosexuality. Many heterosexuals, though, go through programs in various religiously based groups to help them manage their experiences of lust or other distorted experiences of sexual desire, or to work through experiences of sexual trauma.

There are many such paraprofessional groups throughout the country and the world. The most prominent are groups affiliated with Exodus International, groups affiliated with Homosexuals Anonymous, and groups affiliated with Courage. There are also many other independent religion-based ministries, including Redeemed Life and Pastoral Care

---

[39]Mark A. Yarhouse, "Group Treatments for Homosexuals Seeking Change," *Journal of Psychology and Theology* 26 (1998): 256.

Ministries, for example.[40] Many of these ministry-based groups state or suggest that change of sexual orientation can occur, although many leaders or representatives will share that many people move out of homosexual behavior and self-identification into celibacy, which they argue is a good in and of itself, while others pursue change to heterosexuality. Other faith-based support groups do not attempt change of orientation; rather, they encourage and support efforts at celibacy.

Exodus International is an umbrella organization for over 100 religion-based support groups in North America. According to Joe Dallas, past president of Exodus International, homosexuality is a learned behavior related to relational deficits of some kind. He writes in his book *Desires in Conflict*[41] that homosexuals can experience change in any one of several areas, including behavior and frequency and intensity of same-sex attraction. Many affiliated ministries appear to conceptualize homosexuality in a similar way, although the groups vary as to who they service and whether they pursue change of orientation or emphasize decreased homosexual identification and behavior.

As the ads in the major newspapers suggest, anecdotal reports of change abound. There have been few published outcome studies of Exodus International-affiliated groups, however. One recent attempt to measure successful change of orientation has produced interesting results. Kim Schaeffer and his colleagues from Point Loma Nazarene University report findings on 184 males and 64 females from Exodus-affiliated ministries.[42] They found on measures of both feeling and behavior that "participants rated their current sexual orientation [i.e., after involvement in the attempt to change sexual orientation] as significantly more heterosexual than when they were 18 years of age."[43] Another finding was that the more heterosexuality that was reported, the better the self-reported mental health, including higher levels of happiness, positive outlook on life and self-acceptance,

---

[40]Mark A. Yarhouse, Lori A. Burkett and Elizabeth M. Kreeft, "Competing Models for Shepherding Homosexual Persons" (paper presented at the Christian Association for Psychological Studies National Conference, Colorado Springs, Colo., April 1999).

[41]Joe Dallas, *Desires in Conflict: Answering the Struggle for Sexual Identity* (Eugene, Ore.: Harvest House, 1991).

[42]Kim W. Schaeffer, Ree Ann Hyde, Thaya Kroencke, Blanca McCormick and Lynde Nottebaum, "Religiously-Motivated Sexual Orientation Change," *Journal of Psychology and Christianity* 19 (2000): 61-70.

[43]Ibid., p. 64.

and lower levels of tension, depression and level of paranoia.[44] Many participants had also been involved in therapy to change sexual orientation, and results from this study did not find evidence for the effectiveness of these experiences in therapy for changing sexual orientation. Involvement in professional therapy in addition to Exodus group involvement, in other words, did not appear to increase the likelihood of change occurring. This research team also reported that religious motivation predicted a person's current sexual orientation, as those who were highly motivated reported experiencing more heterosexuality.[45] A follow-up study[46] one year later suggests that religious motivation is also associated with efforts to abstain from physical homosexual contact (referred to as "behavioral success," which was reported at a rate of 60.8% of the 102 males in the follow-up study and 71.1% of the 38 females in the follow-up study).

Homosexuals Anonymous (HA) represents approximately fifty chapters throughout North America. HA follows the general format of Alcoholics Anonymous but is more overtly Christian. They have fourteen steps that roughly parallel AA with some specific adaptations for homosexuality and specific to Christian faith.[47]

---

[44]These findings are particularly interesting in light of claims from some mental health professionals that efforts to change are harmful to gay and lesbian persons. This is an especially complicated issue. The findings from this study show an association between more heterosexuality and various measures of mental health; however, another study by Nottebaum, Schaeffer, Rood and Leffler reported that, when compared to a those who rejected their homosexuality and were involved in Exodus-affiliated ministries, those who accepted their homosexuality reported experiencing better mental health on measures of happiness, self-acceptance, paranoia and loneliness. See Lynde J. Nottebaum, Kim W. Schaeffer, Julie Rood, Deborah Leffler, "Sexual Orientation: A Comparison Study," *The International Journal for the Psychology of Religion* (manuscript submitted for publication).

[45]Schaeffer and his colleagues are right in pointing out that this finding should be interpreted with caution. We would not want to send the message that those who do not experience change are simply not motivated to change. At the same time, religious motivation may be an important factor in deciding whether to pursue change.

[46]Kim W. Schaeffer, Lynde Nottebaum, Patti Smith, Kara Dech and Jill Krawczyk, (1999), "Religiously-Motivated Sexual Orientation Change: A Follow-Up Study," *Journal of Psychology and Theology* 27, no. 4 (1999): 329-37.

[47]The fourteen steps of HA are as follows: (1) we admitted that we were powerless over our homosexuality and that our emotional lives were unmanageable; (2) we came to believe the love of God, who forgave us and accepted us in spite of all that we are and have done; (3) we learned to see purpose in our suffering, that our failed lives were under God's control, who is able to bring good out of trouble; (4) we came to believe that God had already broken the power of homosexuality and that he could therefore restore our true person-

The goal of HA is to change sexual orientation, which, they claim, is a *life-long process* (in the same sense that recovery from alcoholism is a lifelong process in AA). Reorientation is pursued by drawing on a person's relationship with God and with others. Support is provided through regular meetings that emphasize reading of Scripture, prayer and the grace of God. As was true of Exodus International-affiliated groups, there are no published outcome studies at this time to confirm the effectiveness of HA, although there are a number of testimonials of change. (This is also consistent with AA, where there has historically been great difficulty establishing the effectiveness of support groups due to high dropout rates and fluid membership.)

Courage is affiliated with the Roman Catholic church, and in contrast to HA and many of the Exodus International-affiliated groups, Courage does not pursue change of sexual orientation. (Again, it should be noted that many Exodus International-affiliated groups and independent groups promote celibacy and recovery from sexual struggles without necessarily promoting or promising change of orientation.) Courage does not discourage those who want to attempt change of orientation (and have the resources to do so) from doing so.

According to Fr. John Harvey,[48] Courage began in New York City in

---

hood; (5) we came to perceive that we had accepted a lie about ourselves, an illusion that had trapped us in false identity; (6) we learned to claim our true reality that as humankind, we are part of God's heterosexual creation and that God calls us to rediscover that identity in Him through Jesus Christ, as our faith perceives Him; (7) we resolved to entrust our lives to our loving God and to live by faith, praising Him for our new unseen identity, confident that it would become visible to us in God's good time; (8) as forgiven people free from condemnation, we made a searching and fearless moral inventory of ourselves, determined to root out fear, hidden hostility, and contempt for the world; (9) we admitted to God, to ourselves, and to another human being the exact nature of our wrongs and humbly asked God to remove our defects of character; (10) we willingly made direct amends wherever wise and possible to all people we had harmed; (11) we determined to live no longer in fear of the world, believing that God's victorious control turns all that is against us into our favor, bringing advantage out of sorrow and order from disaster; (12) we determined to mature in our relationships with men and women, learning the meaning of a partnership of equals, seeking neither dominance over people nor servile dependency on them; (13) we sought through confident praying and the wisdom of Scripture for an ongoing growth in our relationship with God and a humble acceptance of his guidance for our lives; and (14) having had a spiritual awakening, we try to carry this message to homosexual people with a love that demands nothing and to practice these steps in all our lives' activities, as far as lies within us.

[48]John F. Harvey, *The Homosexual Person: New Thinking in Pastoral Care* (San Francisco: Ignatius, 1987), p. 141.

1980 and holds to the following five goals:

1. to live chaste lives in accordance with the Roman Catholic Church's teaching on homosexuality

2. to dedicate one's entire life to Christ through service to others, spiritual reading, prayer, meditation, individual spiritual direction, frequent attendance at Mass, and the frequent reception of the sacraments of Penance and of the Holy Eucharist

3. to foster a spirit of fellowship in which one may share with others one's thoughts and experiences and so ensure that no one will have to face the problems of homosexuality alone

4. to be mindful of the truth that chaste friendships are not only possible but necessary in celibate Christian life and to encourage one another in forming and sustaining them

5. to live lives that may serve as good examples to other homosexuals

Courage reminds the Christian that people can have a full, rich life and be celibate. Unfortunately, Courage does not publish outcome data that might further our understanding of people's experiences in their groups.

We have been discussing Exodus, HA and Courage, the major national religious ministry groups. One notable scientific study of the effectiveness of a change ministry was performed with an independent Pentecostal church ministry unaffiliated with the above groups. In the late 1970s Pattison and Pattison[49] came into contact with a Christian Pentecostal "hot-line crisis program" that sought to help homosexuals leave the gay lifestyle, change to heterosexuality via "religiously mediated" means and mature as Christians. The Pattisons reviewed with the church staff 300 cases in search of individuals who had, in the estimation of the staff, "changed sexual orientation." Thirty such cases were identified and contacted for extensive interviewing; of the 30 contacted, 11 agreed to fully cooperate with the evaluation.[50]

---

[49]E. Monsell Pattison & Myrna L. Pattison, "Ex-gays: Religiously Mediated Change in Homosexuals," *American Journal of Psychiatry* 137 (1980): 1553-62.

[50]Haldeman, in his bitingly dismissive review of this study, states "The Pattisons do not explain their sampling criteria, nor do they explain why 19 of their 30 subjects refused follow-up interviews" (p. 224). On the one hand, Haldeman does have a valid point; it is curious that 19 refused interviews and equally curious that the Pattisons give us no indication of why. On the other hand, Haldeman is incorrect in stating that sampling criteria

The Pattison study did an excellent job of using widely respected methods of gathering data on its 11 subjects. Nine of the 11 had been exclusively homosexual ("6" on the Kinsey scale) before their work with the ministry, and after that work, five reported being exclusively heterosexual (Kinsey "0"), with three reporting some incidental homosexual feeling or behavior (Kinsey "1"), and three reporting "definite same-sex response but strong and predominant reaction to the opposite sex" (Kinsey "2").[51] The group averaged having been out of the homosexual lifestyle and identified as heterosexual for four years at the time of the evaluations. Six of the 11 were married, with most reporting their marriages to be "very happy." Most of the men reported some continuing occurrence of homosexual dreams, fantasies or impulses. Most reported fairly low incidence of negative psychological/emotional symptoms. The Pattisons obtained concurring reports from church staff and spouses for some of the subjects in the study. This study does appear to provide definitive evidence that change is possible for some individuals; the fact that the sample pool was 11 out of 300 reviewed does raise serious concerns about how often radical change is likely to occur.

The NARTH Study
The National Association for Research and Therapy of Homosexuality (NARTH) formed a number of years ago to challenge the growing broad acceptance of homosexuality in the mental health professions and the growing rejection of the idea that homosexuality can be changed.[52] NARTH recently produced a study[53] of the change experience for a large number of persons seeking change and of therapists who try to help

---

were not explained; the criteria were simple—select individuals who had changed orientation. It is possible that the 19 nonparticipants refused because they had not really changed and were threatened by the prospect of close scrutiny. An alternative hypothesis would be that they did not desire to relive a painful past with a stranger. Douglas C. Haldeman, "The Practice and Ethics of Sexual Orientation Conversion Therapy," *Journal of Consulting and Clinical Psychology* 62 (1994): 221-27.

[51]Pattison and Pattison, "Ex-gays," p. 1554.

[52]NARTH can be contacted at <www.narth.org> or via Dr. Joseph Nicolosi at 818-789-4440.

[53]NARTH, "A Survey of Sexual-Orientation Change" (press release dated May 17,1997, study undated, available at <www.narth.org> or via Dr. Joseph Nicolosi at 818-789-4440).

individuals change. We did not discuss the study in earlier sections because methodologically it does not fit in any other category. NARTH sought research participants of two sorts: it sought individuals "who had experienced 'some degree of change' " and counselors who attempt to facilitate such change by advertising in newsletters of change support groups (such as the religious groups we just discussed) and via announcements at conferences for such individuals. Like the Pattison study this study was attempting to document that change can happen and sought a suitable subject pool that would illustrate that fact.

Eight hundred fifty-five persons who had changed or who were seeking such change responded to the survey. As a group they tended to be well educated, male, white and devoutly religious. The average age of awareness that they had "homosexual tendencies" was age 12.4. Interestingly, 503 reported having had a childhood homosexual contact at an average age of 10.9 years with the person initiating that contact being an average age of 17.2 years. Survey respondents rated their sexual orientation before treatment began and at the time of the survey. Before the change process 37% reported being exclusively homosexual (Kinsey "6"), 31% reported being a Kinsey "5," 22% were Kinsey "4" and 9% ranging down throughout the rest of the scale. After the change effort 15% reported being exclusively heterosexual (Kinsey "0"), 18% reported themselves to be almost exclusively heterosexual (Kinsey "1"), 20% more heterosexual than homosexual (Kinsey "2"), 11% equally homosexual and heterosexual (Kinsey "3"), 23% more homosexual than heterosexual (Kinsey "4"), 8% almost entirely homosexual (Kinsey "5") and 5% exclusively homosexual (Kinsey "6"). The researchers reported separate statistics for those who reported being exclusively homosexual before treatment began to see if these individuals obtained less help from the therapeutic process; the results suggested that the success rates in this group were similar to the whole group. The participants reported substantial decreases in "homosexual thoughts," masturbation to gay pornography and overt homosexual behavior. Eight hundred thirty-eight participants had obtained some sort of reorientation therapy (over an average span of 3.3 years); 159 had not obtained such therapy. An overwhelming 99% reported believing that homosexual orientation can be changed.

The responses to the therapist survey, perhaps predictably, indicated that the therapists were confident that homosexual orientation can be changed and that they are capable of assisting with that process of change.

Criticisms of Change Programs

There is not a complete professional consensus on how to interpret either the empirical research on change programs or the proliferation of religion-based support groups for those who are attempting to come out of the gay lifestyle or pursue change. As the reader will have noticed, no new original empirical research of real merit has emerged on the question of whether homosexuality can be changed in many years. Some view this as indicating that positive results cannot be found honestly. Others argue that it is impossible to obtain funding to conduct and publish a credible study given how politicized the topic has become.

Douglas Haldeman, past president of the Division for the Psychological Study of Lesbian, Gay and Bisexual Issues in the American Psychological Association, offers the most comprehensive critique[54] of the "conversion" literature to date, one that is unfailingly negative. Haldeman presents in distilled form the types of criticisms of the research we have cited above that a person encounters in reading broadly in the psychological and church literature.

As we begin critiquing his critique, we would note his tendency to argue in an ad hominem fashion; that is, he demeans the conversion literature by describing the various studies as, for instance, "founded on heterosexual bias" and "homophobia." Such blanket criticisms, sprinkled throughout his article, are hardly informative. Rather, they come across as vacuous. Reviewers ought to assess methods, findings and arguments, not the character or motivations of other researchers. We will not contribute to the advance of our knowledge by pointing and yelling "homophobe!" (the person who is afraid of homosexuals) any more than we will by yelling "homophile!" (the person who is attracted to homosexuals).

Haldeman implies that reports of successful change are simply false or fraudulent, that those patients who are said to have changed merely told the researcher therapists what they wanted to hear even though they never really changed at all. He used this sort of argument when he dis-

---

[54]Haldeman, "Practice and Ethics," pp. 221-27.

missed claims of religious healing of sexual orientation (particularly the study of Pattison and Pattison, 1980). The basis for his dismissal was anecdotes (of the following sort: "I know someone who was classified as a success in that study but who did not really change"). We recognize that it is within the realm of possibility that some clients said they changed when they did not. There may be reasons for homosexual clients who are not experiencing change to feign progress so that they could discontinue therapy without disappointing or confronting their therapist. Haldeman's charge of fraud is within the realm of possibility. On the other hand, there is no *evidence* to support Haldeman's charge, and it verges on solipsism. If we accept such a charge, is there any reason to believe that anyone who has ever gone through psychological treatment has told the truth about the changes they have made? Can we ever know anything?

Further, anecdotes of this kind carry little weight in the scientific community for evaluating therapy outcomes, either for or against change. Empirical researchers into psychotherapy outcomes and outcomes from drug trials have trained aversions to anecdotes, positive or negative. For any treatment approach, stories will get around about how the approach worked wonders and about how it failed miserably. What counts are not anecdotes but data. If Haldeman finds it convenient to dismiss anecdotal reports of positive outcomes (change of orientation or healings), then why should his anecdotes of either fraud or failure be given any credence? He cannot have it both ways.

Haldeman does offer two substantive points of criticism of the change literature. First, Haldeman criticizes the therapeutic and religious conversion literature as naively anchored in rigid categories of "gay" and "straight." He suggests that this has led researchers in the past to declare a person "converted" to heterosexuality when, for instance, they show even the slightest capacity for or interest in heterosexual sex. He argues that the categories of homosexual, heterosexual and bisexual are a fluid continuum for many, a continuum on which persons can move back and forth.

This is an important consideration. There really is no consensus as to how to categorize sexual orientation and self-identification, but he is right nonetheless that researchers have not used much creativity, rigor or objectivity in their research definitions of homosexual orientation.

Nevertheless, Haldeman only applies his logic in criticizing the conversion literature and never in criticism of the gay-affirming literature that proclaims change to be impossible. For instance, he describes heterosexuals as coming out as "lesbian or gay later in life" but fails to describe (and seems to allow no possibility of) similar shifts in the other direction (i.e., gays moving toward heterosexuality). Can't it go both ways? Is this because he is already committed to a belief in homosexuality as unchangeable? He only admits (seemingly grudgingly) that homosexual persons might later "engage in heterosexual relationships for a variety of personal and social reasons." The reader of his argument is left with the impression that real change can occur as a person moves toward homosexuality but that movement in the other direction is always superficial and ingenuous. The implication is that "coming out" after a period of heterosexuality is a revelation of one's true sexual identity, while embracing heterosexual behavior after living in the gay lifestyle is a "mere" change of behavior. Haldeman cannot have it both ways.

One further wrinkle on this issue of how one defines sexual orientation. Haldeman's dismissal of all claims of change forces us to conclude that his method is basically this: he examines past research and concludes, *based on his prior commitment to the belief that homosexuality cannot be changed*, that any evidence of change must necessarily have occurred in nonhomosexual (that is, bisexual) patients. Simply put, Haldeman implies time and again that naive and homophobic researchers must have made bad categorizations of their research patients, mixing homosexuals, bisexuals and others. He then implies that any change that did occur must have occurred in the bisexuals that must have been mixed in with the "real homosexuals."

A second point of critique is that Haldeman criticizes change of sexual behavior alone as trivial and not indicative of a more fundamental change of orientation. He criticizes another author who describes the change process away from homosexuality as an "adaptation" that allows homosexual persons to function in heterosexual marriages while homosexual fantasies and behaviors are never really eradicated (the same position we developed for McConaghy earlier). In Haldeman's view any continued experience of same-sex attraction or action is taken as indication of treatment failure.

Again, this criticism of the change literature is partially valid, in that mere behavior change (e.g., the lesbian wife who endures sexual intercourse with her husband by engaging in homosexual fantasy) falls short of a true change of orientation. But two responses to this argument seem important to make. First, this position fails to allow for change to be a process of any kind. Haldeman would have us rush to the judgment that treatment has been a failure when any vestige of homosexual attraction remains.

Further, given how deeply rooted and pervasive we must understand homosexual orientation to be, surely it is an overly high standard of success to demand that treatment of any sort eradicate all vestiges of homosexual attraction and firmly establish heterosexual desire to be deemed successful. Such a high standard would never pass the test for other human conditions. We would not declare alcoholism treatment to be a failure on the basis of some continuing attraction to or even occasional relapses into alcohol consumption. Neither would we declare treatment for depression unsuccessful on the basis of a treated person needing to combat tendencies to reexperience depression. Haldeman's easy dismissal of change reports on the basis of some continuing experiences of same-sex desire, fantasy or even behavior seems impossibly harsh.

Let us close this section with a brief discussion of a crucial issue implicit in Haldeman's analysis but which he does not make explicit. In this and other articles, subtle perspectives are presented suggesting that the older literature on change of homosexual orientation is *especially* bad, especially sloppy, especially worthy of our contempt for its sloppy and deficient methodology. It is interesting to compare the present measures with those of (what are regarded as) respected and successful change methods or positive outcomes for conditions other than homosexuality. For example, in a widely used textbook on family therapy (published in 1998), Michael Nichols and Richard Schwartz[55] discuss empirical support for the use of structural family therapy, a popular and widely used approach in working with families. One study that is cited as evidence for the effectiveness of structural family ther-

---

[55]Michael P. Nichols and Richard C. Schwartz, *Family Therapy: Concepts and Methods,* 4th ed. (Boston: Allyn and Bacon, 1998), pp. 266-67.

apy is a small study (53 families) where children in 43 of the families were "greatly improved," two were "improved," and three showed "no change."[56] These global and vague categories are not unlike those used in the empirical studies cited to support the efficacy of change interventions for homosexuals seeking change. It is possible that the political climate against conservative religion makes some research acceptable to cite as support, while research on homosexuality receives much more scrutiny.

A related issue is whether self-report of change is clinically useful or valid. Often pro-gay advocates dismiss the research conducted during the 1950s-1970s because so much of it relied on therapist- or self-report of change.[57] The reader is left to assume that researchers today (or even back then) have much more sophisticated and objective methodologies and higher standards for measuring change. However, in a presentation of manualized treatment protocol for Attention Deficit Hyperactivity Disorder (ADHD) and Oppositional Defiant Disorder (ODD),[58] a prominent researcher shared (with us) some of the behind-the-scenes realities of trying to have a treatment program empirically validated. In a report on a pilot study and larger study of a combined behavioral modification and communication training program, the researcher discovered that when compared to a behavior modification/parent-training program (as well as structural family therapy, at least in the pilot study), neither program was found to be effective as measured by objective data (it should also be noted that, for ethical reasons, the Human Subjects Review Board would not allow the use of a control group). The families, however, reported improvement across several domains. In other words, the intervention was successful according to self-report but not according to objective measures of change. Was the intervention successful? Does it depend upon whom you ask? This study was done in a research setting with stringent methodology by a highly respected research team.

---

[56]Ibid., 266.

[57] Haldeman, "Practice and Ethics," pp. 221-27.

[58]Gweneth Edwards, "Birth of an Empirically-Supported Treatment Program: Behavior Management and Problem-Solving Communication Training for Families of Teens with ADHD and Oppositional Defiant Disorder" (presentation at the doctor of psychology program 1998-1999 colloquia series, Regent University, January 29, 1999).

The program was not empirically validated, but it was manualized (which means it has been published in a book or manual), and this gives it the appearance of being a scientifically supported intervention for ADHD and ODD adolescents.

In what *meaningful ways* then are the early studies on homosexuality radically different? Most did not utilize control groups. It would be ideal if they did, but most did not, and this is true even today of many outcome studies on a variety of disorders. Many intervention studies do not use control groups for ethical reasons. Similar to the pilot study and research study mentioned above, many individual and group treatments for homosexuality conducted in the 1950s-1970s produced change as indicated by self-report and therapist report. Some of those experiences were verified by objective data, although not all.

Even in the light of Haldeman's criticisms we would argue that the weight of the evidence suggests that change is possible for some. The absolute claim that homosexuality is immutable or unchangeable needs only one case of change to lead us to conclude that homosexuality is not always immutable, that it is in fact changeable, and it would be fantastic to believe that no such cases have been reported in this change literature.

Professional Issues

A word about the professional and ethical implications of this analysis for how Christian psychologists, psychiatrists and other mental health professionals are to act toward persons seeking the possibility of change.

One of the professional and ethical issues we must examine is that of *competence*, which has to do with level of education, training and supervised experience for working with a particular population. Mental health professionals seeking to build competence in this area should be aware of major content areas, including the four we are discussing in this book (prevalence of homosexuality, origins of homosexuality, whether homosexuality can be changed, and the status of homosexuality as a psychopathology).

Another concern is that mental health professionals can only sustain the right to seek treatment if they uphold the right not to seek treatment. This raises the issue of when to refer a client if the therapist is unable to help or is uncomfortable with the requested direction for treatment.[59]

Despite these professional issues it is increasingly important to recognize that clients have the "right to choose" treatment for homosexuality, the right to seek to change their orientation. Every professional organization's ethical code draws attention to a client's ability to function autonomously and make informed decisions about his or her treatment. It is important that Christian psychologists and counselors are up front with clients about the research in this area, including the dearth of studies with sophisticated methodology that support change of orientation. We would argue that clinicians should provide clients a form of *advanced informed consent* to treatment, which includes (but may not be limited to) a discussion of the following:

1. hypotheses as to what is causing their problems (including etiology of same-sex attraction and the subjective experience of distress reported by a particular client)

2. professional treatments available, including success rates and definitions and methodologies used to report "success"

3. alternatives to professional treatment, including reported success rates and the relative lack of empirical support for claims of success

4. possible benefits and risks of pursuing treatment at this time

5. possible outcomes with or without treatment (and alternative explanations for possible outcomes)[60]

Clients benefit from being informed about the nature of the work they would do in therapy, as well as the research that support the likelihood that their treatment goals would be met. It is also important to be realistic with clients about expectations for change based upon the literature we have reviewed above.

Many mental health organizations have passed resolutions opposing

---

[59]We are repeating an argument we first made in Mark A. Yarhouse and Stanton L. Jones, "The Homosexual Client," in *Christian Counseling Ethics: A Handbook for Therapists, Pastors and Counselors,* ed. Randolph K. Sanders (Downers Grove, Ill.: InterVarsity Press, 1997), pp. 139-60. In the discussion of whether or not to refer, we drew on material by Corey, Corey and Callanan and made application to Christian counselors who work with homosexual clients without referencing the original resource. We encourage the reader to see Gerald Corey, Marianne Schneider Corey and Patrick Callanan, *Issues and Ethics in the Helping Professions,* 5th ed. (Pacific Grove, Calif.: Brooks/Cole, 1998).

[60]Mark A. Yarhouse, "When Clients Seek Treatment for Same-Sex Attraction: Ethical Issues in the 'Right to Choose' Debate," *Psychotherapy* 35 (1998): 252

reorientation or reparative therapies for homosexuals, including the American Psychological Association (APA) and the American Counseling Association (ACA).[61] Although these resolutions fall short of calling reorientation therapy unethical, they are certainly intended to discourage this therapy option. However, in an interview intended to clarify the APA's resolution on reorientation therapy, Martin Seligman and Raymond Fowler, both past presidents of the APA, encouraged the public and the press to reread the resolution and see that the APA holds high regard for a person's right to choose reorientation therapy.[62]

Despite resolutions intended to discourage the use of reorientation therapy, members of the APA, ACA and other mental health organizations continue to provide treatment to change same-sex behavior, fantasies or orientation. For example, Jordan and Deluty recently published a small survey of mental health professionals in which 11% reported using interventions to change clients' homosexual orientations (the most commonly used intervention was psychodynamic psychotherapy).[63] Similarly, we noted above that MacIntosh recently published results from a survey of over 1,200 psychoanalysts, where respondents reported working with over 200 homosexual persons who experienced change of sexual orientation. MacIntosh's large numbers suggest that many clinicians continue to provide therapy to those who experience same-sex attraction and seek change.

---

[61]According to the National Association for Research and Treatment of Homosexuality, the groups opposing reparative therapy include: American Academy of Pediatrics, American Federation of Teachers, American Medical Association, American Psychiatric Association, American Psychological Association, The Interfaith Alliance, National Association of School Psychologists, National Association of Social Workers, National Association of Secondary School Principles, National Education Association, New Ways Ministries and People for the American Way <www.narth.com/docs/acaresolution.html>.

[62]National Association for Research and Treatment of Homosexuality, "Some Clarifications about the Psychological Association's Resolution on Reparative Therapy" (available at <www.narth.com/docs/clarifications.html>).

[63]Interestingly, Jordan and Deluty found no differences between psychologists who received their degree before 1970 and after 1978 in either their views of homosexuality as a disorder or their use, or support of the use, of techniques to change sexual orientation, this despite the decision by the American Psychiatric Association in 1973 to remove homosexuality as a psychopathology from its official nomenclature of mental disorders. Karen M. Jordan and Robert H. Deluty, "Clinical Interventions by Psychologists with Lesbians and Gay Men," *Journal of Clinical Psychology* 51 (1995): 448-56.

There are also highly regarded specialists in human sexuality who write about interventions to manage homosexual feelings or behaviors or diminish anxiety about heterosexual behaviors. Whether we consider the silenced professionals who provide treatment but who do not publish outcome studies, or the highly regarded specialists who recognize the effectiveness of interventions to manage thoughts and behaviors, there is no doubt that some professionals continue to provide services to those who are dissatisfied with their experiences of same-sex attraction and seek change.

Conclusion on Change

What can be concluded from the change literature? We do not share the optimistic and seemingly universal generalization of some conservative Christians who seem to imply that anyone with any motivation can change, if change is taken to mean complete alteration of sexual orientation to replace homosexual with heterosexual erotic orientation. Even the most optimistic empirically grounded spokespersons for change by psychological means say that change is most likely when motivation is strong, when there is a history of successful heterosexual functioning, when gender identity issues are not present, and when involvement in actual homosexual practice has been minimal. Change of homosexual orientation may well be impossible for some by any natural means. Yet the position that homosexuality is unchangeable seems questionable in light of reports of successful change.

In informal church dialogue, reports of change by psychological or supernatural means are often dismissed by anecdotes such as "I tried that ministry (therapy), and it was a complete failure. I know lots of people who claimed to change by that means, but they are now out in the gay lifestyle!" Yet it is standard in professional circles to recognize that such anecdotes have no power to either establish or discredit the success of a change method. In that light, it is troubling that the many Christian ministries that attempt to provide opportunities for growth and healing for the homosexual person rarely if ever study and report their success rates.

Relevance to the Moral Debate

What is the formal relevance of change to the moral debate? The conviction in the Christian tradition that homosexual practice is immoral calls on those who are inclined to such behavior to demonstrate obedience to God's revealed will and avoid such behavior. Historically, the church has taught that we are all to strive for obedience to a biblical sexual ethic of chastity in heterosexual marriage or celibacy outside of marriage.

So what is the relevance for this research for the church's moral deliberations? Several questions must be addressed: Change by what methods? Change into what?

Does the church have any stake in the whole debate about whether homosexuals can change via psychotherapy or other natural means? It is not clear that this matter is really crucial to our ethical system as Christians. Christians believe in sin and believe that human beings are helpless to rid themselves of sin. It is only through God's grace that we embark on the journey of combating and overcoming sin. At times the debates about counseling and the homosexual make it sound like the church has no right to believe that homosexual action is immoral unless psychotherapy works. What was the state of our moral system then when psychotherapy as such did not even exist?

Which leads us to the question of what sort of change we are really pondering. Surely dramatic change, a conversion, to heterosexuality is a wonderful gift to a person seeking change. But when the apostle Paul said "that is what some of you were" (1 Cor 6:11), we have no assurance that he meant that the former "homosexual offenders" were all fully converted to heterosexuality and happily married. Paul himself was a celibate single man, called his condition a blessed one and wished his condition on others. Is it too much to believe then that what Paul had in mind for the former homosexual offenders was chastity in singleness and freedom from their former sexual enslavement to sin?

From this perspective, Christians who contend with homosexuality are not required to change their sexual orientation; nor are they promised such change. It is consistent with the character of God as revealed in the Christian Scriptures to understand that his desire for us is costly discipleship that frees us from being driven by our longings for happiness and personal gratification of our sexual "needs." Indeed, there are powerful messages missing from the "Christian gay-affirming literature":

> Absent are passionate calls to righteousness and to obedience to God's
> revealed will. Gone is the New Testament repugnance for sexual immoral-

ity and an alternative passion for purity. Gone is a vision for the chaste life of singleness as a lifestyle of dignity and delight. Gone is any sense of how our sexuality, and indeed our faith, can serve purposes beyond meeting our own needs. Absent is a vision for how our sexuality must be harnessed and channeled to serve higher ends. Absent is a cautious awareness of just how contaminated our lives are by the fall and by sin, and of how profound is our capacity for self-deception and desperate need for God's guidance in how to live our lives. Missing is any deep awareness, to paraphrase G. K. Chesterton, that no restriction God might place on how we should experience our sexuality is as incredible as the raw awareness of what a miraculous gift our sexuality is.[64]

As a "worst case" scenario let us suppose that change from homosexual preferences or experiences of same-sex attraction by human effort is found to be impossible. Such a finding would not necessarily change fundamental Christian teaching at all, in that God's standard for homosexual persons would continue to be the same as that for all persons. That standard is chastity in heterosexual marriage or celibacy outside of marriage. It may be that the church can no more guarantee healing to homosexuals than it can guarantee marriage to disconsolate single heterosexuals. There are many more single Christian heterosexuals "doomed" to sexual abstinence by the church's "narrow" sexual morality than there are homosexual persons similarly constrained.

The core issue is that the church's stance on homosexual behavior requires only that individuals be able to refrain from homosexual action and find a life of fulfillment in God's own provision in meeting their personal needs and not that they necessarily be able to become heterosexuals. Certainly behavior change is within the realm of that which can be changed, as evidenced by our understanding of autonomy and free will, as well as scientific findings that clearly support change of behavior methods.

Summary

☐ The research on change of sexual orientation is intensely debated today. Most of the research was conducted and published between the 1950s and the 1970s, with an average positive outcome of approximately 30%.

---

[64]Stanton L. Jones, "Identity in Christ and Sexuality," in *Grace and Truth in the Secular Age*, ed. Timothy Bradshaw (Grand Rapids, Mich.: Eerdmans, 1998), p. 105.

☐ Definitions of "positive outcome" vary across studies. Positive outcome has been defined in the following ways: reduced preoccupation with homosexual thoughts, reduced homosexual activity, reduced anxiety about heterosexual functioning, increased heterosexual activity, increased heterosexual fantasy, celibacy, heterosexual marriage and reports of change of sexual orientation from homosexual to heterosexual.

☐ There are a number of methodological limitations to the early studies published on change, including small sample sizes, the reliance on self-report and therapist-report of change, and lack of control groups. However, many of these same methodological limitations plague studies conducted today, so critics should be consistent across all efforts to provide professional interventions to human concerns.

☐ There may be tremendous value in publishing outcome studies of higher quality than have been published to date. Along these lines, collaboration between religion-based ministries and researchers would provide empirical evidence for what homosexual persons can expect upon entering these programs.

☐ Research on change of orientation is not formally relevant to the moral debate in the church, as the church's moral concern is not with changing experiences of same-sex attraction but with how a person chooses to express those inclinations across relationships.

Discussion Questions

1. What are your impressions of the different measures of "positive outcome" in the change literature?

2. How relevant are these reports of "positive outcome" to people who contend with same-sex attraction?

3. Why is informed consent important when someone experiences same-sex attraction and pursues change?

4. How relevant are studies on change to the moral debate in the church?

6

Toward a Christian Sexual Ethic

I take it for certain that the *physical* satisfaction of homosexual desires is sin. This leaves the [homosexual] no worse off than any normal person who is, for whatever reason, prevented from marrying. . . . Our speculations on the cause of the abnormality are not what matters and we must be content with ignorance. The disciples were not told *why* (in terms of efficient cause) the man was born blind (Jn. IX 1-3): only the final cause, that the works of God [should] be made manifest in him. This suggests that in homosexuality, as in every other tribulation, those works can be made manifest: i.e. that every disability conceals a vocation, if only we can find it

—C. S. LEWIS, *IN A LETTER TO SHELDON VANAUKEN*

t the heart of this book is an analysis of the use of science in church debates about the morality of homosexual behavior and the ordination of active homosexuals in church office. Although we began this book with a sketch of a Christian sexual ethic, we would like to develop that further in this closing chapter. What we offer here is a natural extension of our critique. If the misuse of science is intended to steer us away from a traditional Christian sexual ethic, then we may need to take some time to clarify what, in fact, is the traditional Christian sexual ethic, and upon what is it based? The answer to these questions is the focus of this concluding chapter.[1]

There was a time when the seemingly undeniable realities of life

---

[1]This chapter is an adaptation from Stanton L. Jones, "The Ethical Crisis: Sexual Ethics and Contemporary Christian Culture" (a paper presented to the Faculty Faith and Learning seminar, Wheaton College, April 1999).

and culture provided support and even confirmation for what Christians understood to be true about sexual ethics. Those days have passed, as even a partial list of developments of the last century shows:

☐ Effective contraceptive methods have broken the seemingly inextricable bond between sexual action and conception/childbearing, and thus also with family life and parenting.

☐ The breakdown of so many marriages has eroded the expectation that marriage is permanent, and this has contributed to diminished expectations that sex should be reserved for (what was) that one lifelong union of husband and wife.

☐ The explosion of "knowledge" has demystified and in most cases normalized behaviors that were previously hidden in obscurity and that were labeled as deviant or pathological.

☐ Urbanization has fostered the development of subcultures of "sexual minorities," and these groups have, in a societal context that emphasizes individual liberty and entitlement, advanced their claims for popular affirmation and legitimization.

☐ The popular triumph of "essentialism," the view that designations like "homosexual" capture a real essence of a person's very *self*, has led to a popular attitude that acting on our impulses, attractions and desires is essential to personal wholeness and actualization.

☐ The revolution in media technologies has made access to sexually titillating material, which was rarely encountered a century ago, now as easy as a keystroke at a computer keyboard or a button press on a remote control.

☐ The triumph of a "sexually affirming culture" has made laughable our once common standards for discourse, for politeness, for modesty, for respect and for restraint, reducing them to that now most despicable of descriptions, "Puritanical."

☐ The documentation by anthropologists of wide variations in tolerance levels across cultures for what Western Christians had assumed to be universally immoral has eroded confidence in universal morality and encouraged the labeling of such universal claims as patriarchal and imperialistic.

☐ We have experienced a corporate erosion of confidence in and acceptance of, and ever escalating hostility to, any sense that the Bible and Christian tradition should set the parameters for law, ethics and our common vision of virtue.[2]

Of particular concern is the reality that so many people approach the moral debates in the church by reasoning backward from experience to theology. On the basis of their relatively unreflective analysis of their personal experience or that of those dear to them, they adjust their views of biblical commands and of principles of biblical interpretation, their understanding of the meaning of discipleship, their conceptions of what it means to be a sexual, physical person created in the image of God, and eventually their very conceptions of the Good and of God. As one Catholic homosexual man said, "I know I'm telling the truth about who I am. I know that the people around me are telling the truth. If we're telling the truth, then the church's position has to be wrong."[3]

Christian Ethics and Contemporary Ethical Reflection

There are many ways to classify different approaches to ethics today. For simplicity, let us provide a sketch of four major approaches. *Deontological ethics* attempts to identify universal principles that should guide behavioral choices ("It is wrong to lie" and "It is wrong to kill"). The major challenges

---

[2]By the phrase "traditional Christian understanding of sexual ethics," we mean the core judgments of the church throughout the ages on the morality of full sexual intimacy outside of the context of heterosexual marriage. The cultural developments we have just mentioned have all had an eroding effect on the level of general acceptance of that traditional ethic, but we would mention two things that we do *not* mean to assert: (1) It is not our intent to paint all of these developments as negative in and of themselves. There is much good about, for instance, the development of contraceptive methods, of media technologies and of crosscultural study of cultural moralities. (2) It is not our intent to argue that the Christian community has been perfect in its handling of sexuality and sexual ethics, nor that the Christian community cannot and should not learn some things and benefit in some ways from developments in contemporary culture relating to sexuality. In many parts of the Christian world, a traditional ethic has been often paired with unjustifiably negative or fearful views of sexuality, with suffocating prudery, with demonization of homosexual people, with extreme and unfocused guilt, and with deeply ingrained shame. These are terrible problems. In our view, however, if the church allows its traditional (i.e., biblical) ethic to erode in the process of dealing with such concerns, it will have won several small battles but lost the war. Our intention is to help defend that deeper ethic; dealing with the "down side" of the traditional ethic is another topic for another book.

[3]Andrew Sullivan, Catholic author and social commentator, on why he opposes Roman Catholic teachings on homosexuality; quoted in Terry Mattingly's nationally syndicated religion column for April 22, 1998 (received via e-mail from Terry Mattingly).

to the approach include the difficulty of obtaining agreement on what constitutes a universal principle or principles and then the difficulty of establishing a means for weighing various principles in a specific situation. (In your undergraduate Introduction to Philosophy course, you may have been presented the ethical dilemma of hiding Jews during World War II and being asked about it by Nazi Gestapo: Should you tell the truth?)

Utilitarian ethics attempts to guide ethical choice/action by regarding the consequences of a person's choices or actions; the commonly articulated "do that which brings the most good to the most people" is one quick summary of this approach. The major challenges to the approach are summed up in the observation that the judgment of what is "good" is itself not without controversy (e.g., sexual fulfillment) and that the approach gives us no formula by which we can weigh good for me against good for any number of others.

Both of these first two approaches, additionally, have been increasingly criticized for their treatment of isolated choices and actions as right or wrong apart from consideration of character. Stan's youngest daughter wears a WWJD? bracelet (What Would Jesus Do?), and while he is delighted that she actually aspires to ask that question from time to time, he is also acutely aware that she has little chance to do as Jesus might have done unless she becomes more and more of who Jesus was and is, and unless she loses her life in his. To do this requires that we attend to character or "what sort of person should I be?"

Virtue (or *Aretaic*) *ethics* attempts to return to the ancient Aristotelian understanding of ethics that focuses less on "what is the correct or best action?" and more on "what sort of person should I be and what sorts of virtues should I manifest as I live my life and face such situations?" The challenges to virtue ethics are akin to those for deontological ethics—it is difficult to obtain agreement on what constitutes a universally affirmed virtue, and it is difficult to establish a way by which the various relevant virtues are weighed against each other in a specific situation.

Finally, recent commentators discussing gender differences in moral reasoning have spoken of a *relational approach* to ethics, an ethic of relatedness or of loyalty. As with utilitarian ethics, however, a person can be loyal to the relationship only if he or she has a notion of the good (else, how can I know how to direct my loyalty?).

Christian ethics does not reside in any one of these approaches, although none of them are without value. God's special revelation of his will for our lives certainly contains what we must regard as *universal principles* that should guide our actions. The *consequences* of our choices and actions are relevant to our ethical choice, especially as Christian faith informs our understanding of what is good for us and others. Christian commitment demands that we pursue the *virtues* embodied by Jesus Christ and identified in the Scriptures. And if ever we needed a ringing endorsement of a *relationally* grounded ethic, Christ's words "If you love me, you will obey my commandments" provides it for us.

As has been explored by ancient and contemporary ethicists, Christian commitment demands that we add a fifth element to the ethical mix: *divine command*. God says, "Do not commit adultery." He is the rule giver. By virtue of who he is, our proper response to his command is obedience; not obedience *if* we love him, or *if* we understand the principles guiding the command or consequences that follow obedience, or *if* we have developed the virtue of self-control, just obedience. And note that biblical passages relevant to sexuality are a mix of loyalty exhortations ("if you love me. . .") and behavioral commands ("do not do X") and character evaluations ("do not manifest X trait/pattern") and teachings about principles ("do you not know that X?") and teachings about consequences ("those who do X shall not enter the kingdom"). A Christian ethic will be, first, a biblical ethic, responding to the will of our God as revealed in Scripture.

The Core of the Christian Sexual Ethic

What is the Christian sexual ethic? It is at its core

1. the teaching that our sexuality—our embodiedness, our gender and all aspects of what it means to be men and women—is a precious gift from God

2. the teaching that full sexual intimacy is properly experienced only between a man and a woman who are married

3. the teaching that those who are not married should refrain from full sexual intimacy with others

4. the teaching that all persons, married and unmarried, should be characterized by certain virtues that will guide and mold their living out of their sexual natures before God and their fellow men and women

Where do violations of God's will for our sexuality (that is, sexual sin) *rank* among sins? Many believe today that the preoccupation of the Religious Right with sexual sin is peculiar, repugnant, hypocritical and utterly unjustified. Scripture itself seems of two minds on this, a tension that we ourselves might well seek to emulate. Sexual sin, on the one hand, does not seem a singular preoccupation of Scripture, and nowhere is sexual sin elevated to the chief of all sins. For example, in Ezekiel 16:49 the prophet declares that the sin of Sodom and Gomorrah was that their citizens were "arrogant, overfed and unconcerned; they did not help the poor and needy." In other passages such as Jude 1:7 it is clear that sexual perversion was a dimension of the sinfulness of Sodom and Gomorrah, but it was clearly not the only or primary dimension. Also, in the "vice lists" of the New and Old Testaments (e.g., Gal 5:19-21), sexual sins are mixed in with a variety ubiquitous sins such as hatred, envy, divisiveness and even selfish ambition.

Sexual sin, on the other hand, appears to merit special attention in the Bible. Note first Paul's statement in 1 Corinthians 6:18 that we should "flee from sexual immorality." Why? Because "all other sins a man commits are outside his body, but he who sins sexually sins against his own body." We will unpack what this seems to mean later, but here it is sufficient to note that Paul says, with no ambiguity, that sexual sin is in a category of its own, one that makes its avoidance a matter of extra concern. Further, sexual sin is notable for its appearance in almost every list of vices to avoid; for instance, it appears in the minimal moral list for Jewish and Gentile believers in Acts 15:29. Sexual purity was clearly a concern of the early church; over and over we are exhorted to pursue sexual purity.

Understanding Human Sexuality in a Complete Biblical Context

We will now glean what we can from the Scriptures about our fundamental Christian understanding of human sexuality before we try to grapple with sexual morality specifically. [4] It is important to note that the Scriptures present no organized and detailed treatise on sexuality; an organized understanding must be pieced together from many parts of God's revelation to us.

In 1 Timothy 4:1-5 the apostle Paul declares:

---

[4]Some portions of this section are adapted from chapter five and other chapters of Stanton L. Jones and Brenna B. Jones, *How and When to Tell Your Kids About Sex: A Lifelong Approach to Shaping Your Child's Sexual Character* (Colorado Springs: NavPress, 1993).

The Spirit clearly says that in later times some will abandon the faith and follow deceiving spirits and things taught by demons. Such teachings come through hypocritical liars, whose consciences have been seared as with a hot iron. They forbid people to marry and order them to abstain from certain foods, which God created to be received with thanksgiving by those who believe and who know the truth. For everything God created is good, and nothing is to be rejected if it is received with thanksgiving, because it is consecrated by the word of God and prayer.

Though this passage seems on the surface to say little directly about sexuality, this passage is, in condensed form, the best summary of the Christian view of sexuality in the Bible. Reformed thinkers have portrayed Scripture as organized around four major "acts" or phases in the biblical "drama" of God's dealing with his people: Creation, Fall, Redemption and Glorification. The creation was good in every way. The Fall marred the creation, but the reality of God's marvelous creation continues on, modified by but never destroyed by the Fall. Through Jesus Christ's birth, life, death and resurrection God's work of redemption intrudes on the drama and transforms (or begins to transform) the distortions imposed on creation by the Fall. Glorification yet awaits us, but we must conduct our lives in light of the imminence of that reality. Creation-Fall-Redemption-Glorification is an essential scheme through which to see all of life, including our sexuality.

We see this scheme clearly in 1 Timothy 4. The early Christians were in a pitched battle with Gnosticism, which taught that the two essences of the world, physical reality and spiritual reality, were antithetical. According to Gnostic teaching, spiritual reality was good by its nature, and physical reality (the physical world and the physical body—marriage and sexuality in particular) was intrinsically evil. In florid terms, Paul brands such teaching as heresy, focusing on the Gnostic rejection of sex, the most odious (to the Gnostic) dimension of marriage, and of certain types of food. In contrast, these created gifts are "to be received with thanksgiving." Paul approaches the issue of sex starting from creation, declaring that, "everything God created is good." But he acknowledges that the Fall has marred that creation, and that we must, in a sense, "wipe the dirt off" of God's beautiful creation. This is one of the fruits of God's redemptive work, that the beauty of God's original creation can be partially restored when it is "received with thanksgiving" and "consecrated by the word of God and prayer." So Paul in this passage approaches sex *first* from the viewpoint of creation, *second* from the perspective of the Fall and *third* from God's redemptive work. Glorification is not evident as a theme in this passage, but throughout the Scriptures we are exhorted to view our lives in view of eternity, to live in light of Christ's imminent return, and this view touches sexuality in such passages as Paul's commendation of celibacy in 1 Corinthians 7. We next explore aspects of Creation-Fall-Redemption-Glorification, with the first receiving very extended coverage.

Creation. Three particular implications of the doctrine of the creation deserve explicit discussion. First, bodily existence or embodiment must be viewed as a created good by biblical Christians. The doctrine of creation teaches us that, contrary to Gnostic heresy, our bodies are not an accident or a result of the Fall but were God's design from the very beginning. God looked upon Adam and Eve, sex organs and all, ready for sexual union and procreation, and declared them to be "very good." When we look at the creation story, it is important also to note that the first mention of "soul" in the Scriptures suggests that our typical understanding of soul as something that is in contradiction or opposition to physical existence is a terrible misunderstanding. Genesis 2:7 reports that "the LORD God formed the man from the dust of the ground and breathed into his nostrils the breath of life, and the man became a living being." The Hebrew word for "being" is the same word used for soul; in other words, the man became a living soul. Part of Adam's "soulishness" was his physical existence. We do not just have bodies; we are bodies.

This positive view of embodiment is reinforced by other great doctrines and Scripture passages. The doctrine of the incarnation of Jesus Christ (e.g., Jn 1:14; Heb 2:14) supports the goodness of bodily existence. In fact, Hebrews 2 goes on to teach that Jesus was "made like his brothers in every way" (v. 17), from which we can understand that Jesus was a sexual person just like us; if embodiment and sexuality were bad things, the incarnate second person of the Trinity could not have taken that form. Next, the doctrine of our coming resurrection refutes any notion of the evil of bodily existence. First Corinthians 15:35-44, 53-54 (see also Phil 3:20-21) teaches that we will be raised and given new bodies for eternity if we believe in Christ. Contrary to the frequent image of being disembodied ghosts or spirits who will roam in some ethereal soup for eternity, Scripture teaches we will live as bodies, perfected bodies, forever. Beyond these broad doctrines, a number of specific New Testament texts affirm bodily existence. First Corinthians 6:15-20 teaches that "your bodies are members of Christ himself," and clearly Christ would be no part of depravity or evil. Our bodies form Christ's physical presence in the world today. We then learn that our bodies are the "temple of the Holy Spirit" and that we are to "therefore honor God with your body." A temple is a place of blessing and honor in biblical imagery, and to be able to honor God with our bodies, our bodies must be a suitable gift to offer to God, a gift that is pleasing to God by its nature. Romans 12:1-2 reinforces this teaching; here, the word *body* is used as a synonym for the whole person; a person's body is who he or she is, and it is a suitable gift or sacrifice to God.

The biblical concept of the "flesh"[5] is the most troubling problem for a Christian affirmation of our embodiment. Verses such as Galatians 5:19-21, which term a long list of actions that mark those who are not destined to go to heaven as the "deeds of the flesh" (NASB), would seem to force us to look at our bodies as the enemy of our spiritual nature. Many modern conservative Christians lean in this direction when we take biblical warnings about the flesh (e.g., Eph 2:1-3) to mean that physical creation is bad and that our physical bodies are the enemies of our spiritual natures.[6] This interpretation is wrong for a number of reasons. First, the term *flesh* in the Scriptures can mean a variety of things, including: (a) that aspect of the person that is frail and creaturely (e.g., Is 40:6-8), (b) the physical aspect of all it means to be a person (e.g., 1 Tim 3:16, which refers to Christ in the flesh), (c) the "one flesh" union produced by mar-

---

[5]Note that a number of modern translations of the Bible are moving away from using the term flesh because of the confusion suggesting that the body is some sort of special locus of sin. Thus, while the term flesh is commonly used for a variety of meanings in the New American Standard and King James Versions, the term *sinful nature* is used for the same Greek and Hebrew words in the New International Version.

[6]One example of this tendency might be seen in the widely read ancient devotional classic *The Imitation of Christ* by Thomas à Kempis (trans. Leo Sherley-Price [New York: Dorset, 1952] pp. 171-72): "Grant me this great grace, so necessary to my salvation, that I may conquer the base elements of my nature, that drag me down into sin and perdition. Within my being I can feel the power of sin contending against the rule of my mind, leading me away an obedient slave to all kinds of sensuality." Here the life of the mind is pitted against bodily existence (sensuality).

riage (Gen 2:28), (d) those purely human acts of judgment that occur without bringing God into the picture (e.g., 1 Cor 1:26), and (e) the outlook of the whole person oriented toward self and in active rebellion against God.

It is this last meaning that is most important to us here: the "flesh" that we are to reject is not our physical existence, our bodies, but rather our sinful self-centeredness. This interpretation helps us understand why the "vice list" of the "deeds of the flesh" in Galatians 5 contains sins that a reader could attribute to the body (sexual immorality, debauchery, drunkenness) but also sins we would attribute to the mind (selfish ambition), to the emotions (rage, envy) and to the person's spiritual nature (idolatry, witchcraft). Clearly the term *flesh* cannot mean just the body in this passage. Generally, the *fleshly nature* or *old self* (Eph 4:20-24) is the whole person or any part of the person—body, mind, soul, emotions, spirit, will, heart—that is in rebellion against God; flesh then is a code word for the fallen aspect of who we are as persons. In contrast, the *spiritual nature* or *new self* (Eph 4:20-24) is the whole person or any part of the person—body, mind, soul, emotions, spirit, will, heart—that is submitted to God for his cleansing and direction and enabling, the aspect of ourselves that is being redeemed by Christ's work.

The second implication of the doctrine of the creation is that the differentiation of the two genders is affirmed in the biblical creation narrative. Those great words of Genesis 1:27 serve as our fundamental touchstone: "So God created man in his own image, in the image of God he created him; male and female he created them." Female and male, created alike in the image of God, both blessed and declared "very good" by the Creator, differentiated by the sovereign intent of God, created for relationship with one another after their primary relationship with their Maker. Intrinsic to Christian belief is the proper and equal valuing of female and male.

A third implication of the doctrine of the creation, one fundamental to any proper understanding of sexuality, is our relationality. We are relational beings by God's creation design. We are made to love. In some mysterious way, we mirror God's capacity to be one and at the same time three (the doctrine of the Trinity) in our capacity to be separate and yet united both with God and with a spouse. Our sexuality is a tangible and undeniable lesson or reminder to us that we are incomplete in ourselves and made for union with and completion in that which is other than ourselves.

Continuing to explore the doctrine of creation, and turning from sexuality in general to sexual intercourse in particular, we can discern or infer at least four major and good purposes for sexual intercourse from Scripture. *Procreation* is the first purpose mentioned in Scripture. In Genesis 1:28 God blesses his precious creations by urging them to beget children. Some theologians have drawn a parallel between God's creative work and our ability to procreate, suggesting procreation is one way in which our lives are an image or reflection of God's nature and character. *Union* is the second vital purpose of our sexuality. Genesis 2:24 points to the uniting power of sexual intercourse (see Jesus' discussion of this reality in Mk 10:2-12). First Corinthians 6:12-20 is even more explicit, teaching that even casual sexual union such as that of visiting a prostitute results in the uniting of two strangers in some mysterious way. This is the best explanation of Paul's warning that nonmarital sexual intercourse is a sin against the person's own body—his or her body has, with the sexual act, been made one with another in a way that no other human act can accomplish.

Physical gratification and pleasure are a third purpose of our sexuality. In 1 Corinthians 7:1-9 Paul speaks in the most matter-of-fact way about sexual need and the obligation of spouses to meet each other's needs. Proverbs 5 speaks poetically of the beauty of physical love: "May your fountain be blessed, and may you rejoice in the wife of your youth. A loving doe, a graceful deer—may her breasts satisfy you always, may you ever be captivated by her love" (vv. 18-19). And of course the Song of Songs speaks powerfully of the delights of romantic love and physical rapture. Finally, as a fourth purpose we believe that God means to *instruct* us about our incompleteness, our dependence, through our sexuality. In being made men and women who inevitably feel the urge for union with another whom we love, and whose respective physical-genital apparatuses are so obviously complementary, we are taught that we are incomplete in ourselves and that we need union with "The Other" to be truly ourselves. Marriage and physical union, however, can never completely satisfy our need for completion, and hence it is wrong to argue that married people are "complete" while single persons are not. But through our sexuality we are directed, even driven, out beyond ourselves for that completion. Sexuality is then a concrete lesson about universal truth.

One final point related to creation demands attention as we seek a biblical framework for understanding our sexuality. Any theology and ethic of sexuality must necessarily, in the Christian understanding, connect with our theology and ethic of marriage. Marriage is a good, a blessed, part of the created order. Marriage is a place where we live out a covenantal relationship with another human being in a manner like that which God lives out with us. Marriage is also a primary metaphor for God's love of his people as shown explicitly in the living parable of Hosea's pursuit of his adulterous and promiscuous wife Gomer (Hos 1— 3), the rapturous love poem the Song of Songs, which many regard as metaphorical (in part) for Christ's love for his church, and the wedding feast metaphor which Christ used himself in his parables (e.g., Mt 22:1-14; 25:1-13) and which is seen in a vision by the apostle John at the end of his life (Rev 19:6-10). Indeed, Paul says explicitly in Ephesians 5:25-33 that marriage is meant to be an earthly model of heavenly truth, that the mystery of Christ's love of his bride is meant to be reflected in the earthly relationship of the Christian wife and husband. Marriage is not an incidental human construction but a creational reality. Any sexual ethic constructed without a clear connection to a theology of marriage is destined to be deficient.

Fall. We now turn briefly to the impact of the Fall on our sexuality. Shame over their nakedness was the first and most immediate effect of the Fall; though there was nothing wrong with their physical nakedness, Adam and Eve could not bear the vulnerability of nakedness before God or before each other. Shame remains part of our human heritage—beyond shame over what we have done, we feel shame at what we are (and their shame over nakedness is a powerful clue for us of the integral connection of our bodies with who we are as *selves*). Immediately after Adam and Eve sinned, God told them that power and control struggles between the two of them and between women and men forever would be one of the legacies of their choices (Gen 3). The Fall brought the distortions of selfishness and pride into our sexual lives. Disease, pain in childbirth, and death all entered the world and entered our sexual relationships. We became people who could worship sex like an idol rather than treating it properly. We became capable of treating people like objects to be used for our selfish gratification. The motives of rebellion against God—greed, insecurity, anger, possessiveness and others—became part of our sexual experience, and we became capable of becoming enslaved to our lusts. Truly our depravity is total—every tinge of our sexual natures and of our whole natures as persons is tainted with the dye of sin.

Redemption. How is our sexuality to be redeemed from this fallen condition? Finding life in Christ through the forgiveness of our sins is the starting point for the eradication of the effects of sin on all areas of our life, including our sexuality. Paul's words in 1 Timothy 4 teach us the core: "everything God created is good," if it is "received with thanksgiving" and "consecrated by the word of God and prayer." We are to sanctify our sexuality first by receiving forgiveness for what we have done wrong. We are to reclaim the good gift of our sexuality with thanksgiving. And then we are to dedicate our lives to the word of God and to prayer, with the help of the Holy Spirit, to the end of becoming more Christlike, to becoming more of the person whom God meant us to be. And that includes the sexual dimension of each of us—we are to discover and shape our sexuality in the manner God intended us to. We are to accept and delight in the gift of our sexual natures.

Glorification. The astute arguments of Philip Turner[7] give us valuable insights about the implications of glorification for our daily living out of our sexuality. Turner begins with a chilling depiction of the assumptions that are replacing a Christian view of persons, sexuality and morality. Drawing on the work of the philosopher Charles Taylor, Turner argues that we are increasingly assuming, at the deepest level, that who we are as selves is defined (1) inwardly, by our human subjectivity, rather than by anything outward or objective; (2) by how we live in everyday life, rather than by visions of virtue and possibilities; and (3) by the possibilities we possess for successfully wringing personal satisfactions of various sorts from life (i.e., of "self-actualizing," of pursuing and attaining happiness and fulfillment). Morality then becomes secondary to this view of selves, and the most basic moral principles then become the obligation to act to enhance growth and gratification, to protect each person's rights to such pursuit of happiness and growth, and to eliminate suffering since suffering is always an obstacle and frustration of one's rightful growth.

---

[7]Philip Turner, "Sex and the Single life," *First Things*, May 1993, pp. 15-21.

Turner then points out how our view of our sexuality is transformed. He notes the widespread acceptance of the view that our sexuality "in some way defines the inner depths of the self" and that our sexuality is thus fundamental to the very "powers and abilities [of the self which] the self is to discover, develop, and exercise in the course of daily life."[8] It then follows that "denial of one's 'sexuality' is akin to denial of 'oneself' and so also one's basic 'identity.' "[9]

Turner contrasts two essential elements of Christian understanding against this prevailing view (the latter of which we will return to later): (1) that a self, in the Christian view, is not defined solely or primarily by subjectivity but rather by meanings given by God by revelation and worked out in a community beyond the autonomous self, and (2) the belief that our sexuality, particularly the act of sexual intercourse, has meanings and implications that exist independently of what we might think we mean by such acts and that are intrinsic to those acts.[10] This argument, as well as that below, strikes at the heart of popular essentialism.[11]

Now, finally getting to glorification, Turner argues that we will

---

[8]Ibid., p. 17. This is the expanded form of essentialism mentioned in chapter one.

[9]Ibid., p. 17.

[10]These independent or "objective" meanings will be discussed in a few pages. As a preview, the core must be seen as the function that sexual intercourse serves in establishing "one-fleshedness" between the act's participants. That this function exists independent of the meanings and intentions of the participants is the heart of Paul's teaching in 1 Corinthians 6:15-18.

[11]It is common for conservative Christians to dismiss essentialism, saying, "It is wrong to bind a person's identity to his or her sexual orientation, especially when that orientation is other than heterosexual. Those people need to stop identifying themselves first and foremost as a gay or bisexual, and instead found their identity on who they are in Christ (if indeed they are Christians). Sexual orientation is ultimately irrelevant to identity, to a person's *essence*." Turner's argument to this point is partially a more nuanced version of this argument. We share the concerns so expressed and indeed stand against essentialism as articulated in the gay community. But this complaint needs to be nuanced. We would draw from the earlier discussion of the doctrine of Creation and embodiment, particularly regarding our gendered natures and our relational natures, the point that a biblical view of sexuality demands a high view of the importance of gender and of relatedness in human existence. Hence, it actually *is* important that men are men and women are women, and further, our erotic longings (usually heterosexual but never pure) are part both of our relational natures and our gender identities. Hence, to speak of a heterosexual father who is Christian, *part* of his identity before God *is* that he is male, that he loves and experiences sexual passion for his wife, that he has thus been blessed with being a father, and

deal properly with sexuality only when we see it in the context of all of life, which must, in the biblical understanding, include our ultimate and eternal context. "The ethics of sex ought to be placed within the full context of the Christian life and the churches' pastoral ministry. . . . To place sexual relations in this full and more adequate context, Christians ought to understand them as part of the undertaking that encompasses all aspects of their lives. That undertaking is holiness of life and its end is not repression but joy unconfined."[12] As opposed to subjective undertakings defined by the autonomous self's desire for self-actualization, Christians believe that God places before us an objective pursuit defined by him—holiness. Holiness in this life is a calling, in part, of preparation for and partial realization now of what will eventually be ours forever in glorification. To pick up one earlier thread: to the secular mind, suffering is a frustration of a person's rightful pursuit of satisfaction; but to the Christian, suffering (such as the real suffering of sexual disappointment and frustration, and their deeper root, loneliness) is integral to our questing after a goal that only begins when this life ends—holiness, purity, Christlikeness and giving glory to God. In short, we live our sexuality properly only when we live it in light of eternity.

An Expanded Sketch of Christian Sexual Morality

With our foundational understanding of sexuality now made explicit, we return to the specific topic of sexual ethics. It is our aim as Christians to be shaped by the words of Scripture, and so we turn first to the vision we gain of sexual ethics in the Bible. The easiest way to summarize the biblical material is to distinguish those sexual behaviors and behavior patterns that are judged moral or good in Scripture from those judged immoral or evil by specific biblical texts. The sexual behaviors and patterns that are

---

so on. His identity, properly, is not and cannot just be that he is a Christian. Where the popular expression of essentialism goes wrong, it would seem to us, is first in its placing of erotic passion and desire and intimacy too high up the priority scale (thus essentially collapsing gender and relationality into sexual passion), and second, in failing to contend with the truth that much that is fundamental to our identities is *bad*—we are after all, sinful and fallen to the core, and while that is part of our identities, it is not something around which to cultivate an identity.

[12]Turner, "Sex and the Single Life," p. 20.

judged moral in Scripture[13] are sexual intercourse in marriage (1 Cor 7:3; 1 Tim 4:1-5; Heb 13:4) and celibacy (Mt 19:12; 1 Cor 6 and 7). That celibacy is singled out for approval is noteworthy, both for those contemporary singles who feel (often rightly) that American evangelicals are so focused on marriage and the family that their unique contributions and struggles are given short shrift, but also as the best case for establishing that, as fundamental as sexuality generically is to human existence, overt sexual gratification can never be lifted up as a requisite of normalcy.

The sexual behaviors and patterns judged immoral in Scripture are, in rough order of their appearance: adultery (Ex 20:14 and many other passages), incest (Lev 18:6-18; 20:11-22), homosexual intercourse (Lev 18:22; 20:13, Rom 1:26-27; 1 Cor 6:9), bestiality (Lev 20:15-16), rape (Deut 22:23-29), lust (Mt 5:28) and fornication (Acts 15:29; 1 Cor 6:9). To preview later distinctions, sexual intercourse during the woman's menstrual period (Lev 18:19) is condemned, but it does not seem that this is properly termed immoral, and the apostle Paul advises strongly against withholding sexual intercourse in marriage (1 Cor 7:1-7).

There are challenges in making sense of the Bible's teachings about sexual ethics. There are definitional issues (what is fornication? lust?). There are issues of biblical context—what are we to make of Scripture addressing in the same chapter (e.g., Deut 22) instructions of how to handle bird nests (vv. 6-7) and how to handle cases of adultery (v. 22)? What of the Bible seeming to condone polygamy and its silence regarding other sexual behavior possibilities like masturbation or "petting"? What are we to make of the consequences that offend our contemporary sensibilities (e.g., death for adultery [Deut 22:22] or a lifetime sentence of marriage to her rapist for a nonbetrothed virgin who is raped [Deut 22:28-29])? And what of the appearance that the patriarchal structure of Israeli society shaped the rule against adultery on the view that the wife was the *property* of her husband? Resolution of all of these and the other problems is probably impossible and certainly beyond the scope of this chapter.

Interpretation of the Old Testament in particular is aided by observing the distinction between civil, ceremonial and moral law that is affirmed by the Westminster Confession and Catechism and other related Reformation documents. It is asserted that the Old Testament law is a mixture of

---

[13]The passages listed are exemplary and not exhaustive.

these three different types of law. The *moral* law is comprised of the enduring moral standards that are timeless and universal. The *civil* law refers to those dimensions of God's commands that had to do with the ordering of civic culture in Israel, a unique nation that was to be set apart and of one mind in its allegiance to Jehovah and his revealed Law.[14] The *ceremonial* law is comprised of those commands that served to create and foster the religious identity and culture of Israel as distinct from the cultures surrounding them and possibly to prefigure or foreshadow elements of Christ's later work. Consider the following examples: the biblical prohibition against adultery is seen as moral, the death penalty as punishment for adultery in Israeli society is civil law (as are specific standards of evidence and judicial processes that might lead to such a penalty), and the dietary regulations of Israel are ceremonial law.

That these are often intermixed in a most confusing way can be seen by examining Deuteronomy 22, where we find in verse 8 a civil regulation regarding parapets on roofs analogous to our safety building standards, in verses 9-12 ceremonial instructions regarding not mixing things that do not belong together, and in verse 22 a specification that the civil penalty for adultery is death (the moral law against adultery is clearly behind the civil ruling on punishment). In the next chapter of Deuteronomy we see an example of the frankness of the Bible in dealing with human matters in its discussion of the ceremonial implications of emissions of semen and sanitary concerns for fecal material (Deut 23:9-14). It is instructive to note that either the moral or ceremonial law is usually in the background of the civil law, which often consists of regulations on judicial processes and on penalties for violations of the other two types of law.

It is commonly and somewhat simplistically assumed by Christian laypersons that neither the ceremonial nor the civil law are binding on our lives today in any way. The ceremonial law is seen as obsolete because its purposes (whether that of foreshadowing Christ or of forging a distinct

---

[14]Christians who believe in inerrancy must in some way regard that civil law as right and perfect for Israel—it was, after all, revealed by God—but Christians disagree on the enduring relevance of this law for societies two and three millennia later, societies that are pluralistic, democratic, nontheocratic and so forth. Some Christians (varyingly termed Theonomists or Christian Reconstructionists) believe that these laws are still the perfect model of justice and are binding on society today, others that they have no binding relevance for today's governance.

tribal identity for Israel or whatever) were fulfilled, or because it was formally abrogated by Peter's vision in Acts 10:9-23. The civil law of Israel is seen as obsolete because it was and is peculiar to a unique and homogeneous theocratic society at a distinct point in history. By this analysis, for instance, prohibitions on sex during a woman's menstrual period were an artifact of Hebraic ceremonial regulations relating to blood and of no enduring moral consequence. Similarly, the civil penalties for sexual violations may serve to document God's concern for sexual purity but are not a guide for how a church leadership board should punish violations of the moral law. While largely correct, this easy dismissal of the ceremonial and civil law may be a bit *too* easy. For instance, what should Christians who take a strong view of inspiration think about the civil regulations of Israel? How can we escape seeing them as a model of perfect justice if issued from the very mouth of God, and what are the implications of such a view for our role as citizens today?[15]

Synthesis

We return now to the earlier discussion of ethical systems and organize

---

[15]First, let us offer the undefended opinion that the Levitical prohibition against sexual intercourse during the menstrual period is the only biblical law regarding sexual behavior that is wholly a matter of ceremonial regulation and hence no longer binding. Construction of a coherent rationale by which moral, ceremonial and civil laws can be disentangled and relevant contemporary judgments made is beyond the scope of this chapter.

Second, we want to briefly address some of the challenging issues mentioned earlier, mainly to suggest that workable resolutions are at least possible. The developmental character of God's special revelation of his will for our lives is obvious in Scripture. In the New Testament we see a raising of the expectations when, for instance, Christ goes beyond behavioral restrictions (adultery) to condemn even states of the heart (lust). God revealed more and more of his standards to his people as they were ready to understand and live by those standards. This helps us to address polygamy, for example, which (like slavery) is described and regulated in the Scriptures (e.g., Deut 21:15-17) but never approved. The earliest biblical statements about marriage undercut the practice of polygamy: how can a man and a woman become one flesh (Gen 2) when there are six women and one man? Yet God, in his wisdom, chose not to forbid polygamy in early Israelite society but rather determined and willed that it would die out as the Hebrew people grew in number and sophistication in understanding God's will and work among them. The seemingly barbaric story of Onan in Genesis 38, like many examples of polygamy, is best seen in light of the imperative of property-ownership preservation through continuation of family lines, which in turn was essential to the protection in old age of widows and other unmarried women—widows without sons could be forced into prostitution for survival until Israelite society grew in size and economic complexity.

the Christian sexual ethic around those five themes, with extended attention given to the third.

A Christian sexual ethic is

☐ *An ethic of obedience.* Christians are to be people marked by our willingness to submit to the revealed will of God. Once we understand what God has said, we are to be marked by our eagerness to obey, even when we do not understand.

☐ *An ethic of loyalty.* Jesus, in John 14:21, states "Whoever has my commands and obeys them, he is the one who loves me. He who loves me will be loved by my Father, and I too will love him and show myself to him." The apostle John, remembering those words at the end of his life, wrote in 1 John 2:4 "The man who says, 'I know him,' but does not do what he commands is a liar, and the truth is not in him." Loyalty to Jesus demands conformity to his revealed will. Further, when we understand the unifying nature of sexual intercourse (discussed next), loyalty to a current or future spouse demands chastity.

☐ *An ethic of principle.* The core principle that should guide our reasoning about sexual morality, the one most missed in contemporary discussion about this topic, has to do with the nature and purpose of sexual inter-

---

The challenge of the preoccupation of the Old Testament with adultery as a violation of the husband's property rights can be seen in a similar light. Adultery, a man having sex with another man's wife, is punishable by death for both participants (Deut 22:22), while sex with a female slave who is promised in marriage but not yet freed is punishable only by having to make a sin offering (notably, this is still termed a sin; Lev 19:20-22). Some have argued that no penalty or even moral disapproval at all is attached to sex with an unmarried woman in the Old Testament, but this seems untrue. If a young bride was discovered by her new husband to have had sex, she was to be stoned, even though no punishment is mentioned for her premarital partner (Deut 22:22-21). Further, prostitution is termed "wickedness" in Leviticus 19:29, throughout the Proverbs and in other places. Scripture condemns sexual relations by any man with a woman to whom he is not married *even though the civil penalties vary according to marital status.* The lack of civil punishment for the male sexual partners of the unmarried woman (who was presumed to be a virgin, Deut 22:22-21) appears to be an artifact (1) of a social context in which independent dating (with its opportunities for sexual experimentation) did not exist and that prized virginity and the married estate, and hence that actually offered little opportunity for premarital sex to occur; and (2) of a system of jurisprudence that placed great emphasis on the testimony of at least two witnesses (Deut 17:6; 19:15) in cases that could result in the death penalty. In "crimes of passion" there are typically no other witnesses except the paramours, and the testimony of the woman would by itself be insufficient by this testimonial standard to result in the death penalty for the male participant.

course itself. Discussants rarely step back and identify what sexual intercourse is and what it is for. It is presumed that it is simply a biological function or a means of reproduction or an opportunity for pleasure or some other secondary function. Earlier we identified four purposes for sexual intercourse. We would here argue that its most fundamental purpose that conditions the other three purposes is identified in Scripture: *sexual intercourse was made by God to create and sustain one fleshedness in a male-female married couple*. No one has expressed this better than Lewis Smedes, who writes:

> It does not matter what the two people [who are having sex] have in mind. . . . The *reality* of the act, unfelt and unnoticed by them, is this: It unites them—body and *soul*—to each other. It unites them in that strange, impossible to pinpoint sense of "one flesh." There is no such thing as casual sex, no matter how casual people are about it. The Christian assaults reality in his night out at the brothel. He uses a woman and puts her back in a closet where she can be forgotten; but the reality is that he has put away a person with whom he has done something that was meant to inseparably join them. This is what is at stake for Paul in the question of sexual intercourse between unmarried people.
>
> And now we can see clearly why Paul thought sexual intercourse by unmarried people was wrong. It is wrong because it violates the inner reality of the act; it is wrong because unmarried people thereby engage in a life-uniting act without a life-uniting intent. Whenever two people copulate without a commitment to life-union, they commit fornication.[16]

A fundamental dimension to Christian sexual morality is whether or not our actions conform to the creational intent or purpose intended for that act. Earlier we mentioned that Philip Turner asserted that the Christian belief in an objective meaning or meanings of sexual intercourse is pivotal to our ethical reflections; one-flesh union is that objective meaning. Turner correctly argues that if sexual intercourse has no objective and unique meaning, then we have erased the moral significance of sexual intercourse; it has become only one among many other ways to achieve certain desired ends. When sex is just one among many ways to express affection or affirm our worth or whatever, relative and idiosyn-

---

[16]Lewis Smedes, *Sex for Christians*, rev. ed. (Grand Rapids, Mich.: Eerdmans, 1994), pp. 109-10.

cratic meanings become the only vocabulary by which ethical decisions about sex can be made.

□ *An ethic of caution.* The empirical evidence supports the view that sex within biblical parameters is more likely to have beneficial consequences and less likely to have damaging consequences than sex outside of those parameters. Persons who engage in extramarital sex expose themselves to heightened probabilities of experiencing unwanted pregnancy, sexually transmitted diseases and other tangible dangers. It is ironic that many people in America today cohabit before marriage in an attempt to enhance their chances of having a satisfying marriage, when the empirical evidence indicates that cohabitation before marriage increases the likelihood of divorce after marriage and of adultery and diminished sexual satisfaction during marriage.[17]

□ *An ethic of virtue.* The virtues that we are urged to develop in Scripture include self-control, purity, faithfulness, trustworthiness and love. The cultivation of these virtues would make the likelihood of sexual sin diminish.

Scripture is silent on many sexual behavior possibilities; it does not seem to be aiming for exhaustiveness. There are certain sexual behaviors, such as sex with corpses or "gerbiling" (the insertion of live animals into the rectum for sexual stimulation), that are not mentioned in Scripture but which a bit of reasoned extrapolation from the five principles above would suggest to be immoral. There are other behavioral possibilities, such as masturbation, utilization of pornography, contraception and "petting," which merit serious and extended discussion even to arrive at tentative conclusions (though some of these issues are ones on which indecision and ambiguity is not an option for most 14-year-olds).[18] Nev-

---

[17]Michael Bracher, Gigi Santow, S. Phillip Morgan and James R. Trussel, "Marriage Dissolution in Australia: Models and Explanations," *Population Studies* 47 (1993): 403-25; Susan L. Brown and Alan Booth, "Cohabitation Versus Marriage: A Comparison of Relationship Quality," *Journal of Marriage and the Family* 58 (1996): 668-78; Larry L. Bumpass and James A. Sweet, "National Estimates of Cohabitation," *Demography* 26 (1989): 615-25; Alfred DeMaris and K. V. Rao, "Premarital Cohabitation and Subsequent Marital Stability in the United States: A Reassessment," *Journal of Marriage and the Family* 54 (1992): 1778-90; David R. Hall and John A. Zhoa, "Cohabitation and Divorce in Canada: Testing the Selectivity Hypothesis," *Journal of Marriage and the Family* 57 (1995): 421-27.

[18]Stan and Brenna Jones discuss these extensively in various places in *How and When to Tell Your Kids About Sex*.

ertheless, we hope the reader can see how an analysis of the five aspects of a Christian sexual ethic with regard to such cases can help the individual Christian to make a decision before God on how he or she is going to be faithful to God in that area.

The Christian struggling with the question of masturbation, for example, must work out issues of obedience (a challenge when Scripture seems silent on this topic but nevertheless condemns lust), loyalty ("Am I acting as a faithful follower if I masturbate?"), principle (Does masturbation's immediate failure to contribute to life union with a mate indicate that it is a violation of moral law or that it is "developmentally incomplete"?), caution (while masturbation has none of the legendary consequences that are snickered about today—blindness, insanity, hairy palms—we may ask whether the oft-reported guilt and sense of compulsion/bondage associated with it are intrinsic to the act and indicative of its depravity/impurity, or a result of overscrupulosity) and virtue (Is a person who masturbates acting virtuously? Is that person pursuing holiness?).

Challenges to Traditional Christian Sexual Morality

There are, or course, many voices in the church today who would dispute this sketch of sexual morality; we will briefly sketch two different types of revisionist arguments.[19] First, there are approaches that develop alternatives to traditional morality on the basis of arguments rooted in a close reading of the biblical sources themselves. These are, if you will, variant biblical theologies[20] of sexuality; the very popular argument of

---

[19]In presenting these in abbreviated fashion, we will of course verge on presenting caricatures rather than fair characterizations of these arguments. We believe these summaries are accurate though compressed.

[20]For those who may not be familiar with this term, it may be helpful to note that "theology" is done at different "levels." After exegesis of a passage or book of Scripture, we are doing theology when we try to systematize in any way the message that is being communicated. Such theology is, in biblical studies, often done at the book (e.g., the theology of Hebrews) or authorial (e.g., Pauline, Johanine or Petrine theology) levels. When a person moves to the next level, he or she is doing New Testament or Old Testament theology, and at the next level of abstraction dealing with the entire corpus of special revelation, biblical theology. Systematic theology attempts to go beyond biblical theology to "fill in the gaps" and to extend the scope of our theological understandings via human reason, dealing with topics not covered directly by the biblical revelation. Perhaps at the highest level of abstraction we have philosophical theology. It is worth noting that Old

William Countryman in his book *Dirt, Greed and Sex*[21] will serve as an effective example of this tradition. Second, there are approaches that develop their arguments at considerable distance from the specifics of biblical revelation, allowing broader theological (or seemingly theological) themes to drive their conclusions about ethics. A summary of James Nelson's influential book *Embodiment*[22] and of the 1991 majority report of a committee commissioned to study and report on human sexuality in the Presbyterian Church of the USA[23] will serve to illustrate this second approach.

Countryman, in *Dirt, Greed and Sex*, is a fine example of the way that self-declared commitments to fidelity to the biblical revelation are no guarantee that the results of the analysis will be acceptable to traditional Christians, nuanced and sophisticated though the analysis may be. He argues that behind and undergirding all of the biblical texts dealing with sexuality are two ethical principles: purity (hence "dirt" or "dirty") and property (hence "greed").[24] Significantly, for Countryman, it is the principles and not the moral rules based upon them that are ethically binding to some degree. Each of the Old Testament teachings on sexuality are built on one or both of these principles: adultery and incest are property violations (one man stealing or abusing another man's property—his wife or daughter respectively), while sex during the menstrual cycle, homosexuality and bestiality are purity violations (they are abominations or "unclean").

The heart of his argument is the claim that Jesus and the apostles completely abrogated the purity ethic principle and substantially trans-

---

and New Testament theology and biblical theology went through a period of substantial disfavor in the academic theology establishment because both are premised upon a presumption that was questioned or denied by many scholars—that is, that the Bible (or either testament) actually constitutes or manifests a cohesive message. It was argued by many that there is no more of a cohesive message there than there is, say, a literary anthology.

[21]L. William Countryman, *Dirt, Greed and Sex: Sexual Ethics in the New Testament and Their Implications for Today* (Philadelphia: Fortress, 1988).

[22]James B. Nelson, *Embodiment: An Approach to Sexuality and Christian Theology* (Minneapolis: Augsburg, 1978).

[23]Presbyterian Church in the United States of America, *Keeping Body and Soul Together: Sexuality, Spirituality, and Social Justice* (reports to the 203rd General Assembly, pt. 1. Stated Clerk of the General Assembly, Louisville, Ky., 1991).

[24]Note the contrast with the more traditional moral, civil and ceremonial law analytic scheme.

formed the property ethic principle. The purity principle essentially disappears—between Jesus' flagrant and frequent violation of purity standards (healing on the sabbath, consorting with sinners and touching lepers) and Peter's vision of Acts 10, all that is left of the purity code is condemnation of impure attitudes like arrogance or greed. The property code was transformed as the egalitarianism of Jesus and the early church disrupted Hebraic patriarchalism and replaced it with a focus on the Christian fellowship, rather than the biological family, as the focus of fidelity, and with a radical individualism where each person is ultimately his or her own property.

Countryman's system effectively dismisses the previously presumed ethical continuity in presentation and preservation of the moral law between the Old and New Testaments. He is commendably precise about the implications of his analysis: "To be specific, the gospel allows no rule against the following, in and of themselves: masturbation, nonvaginal heterosexual intercourse, bestiality, polygamy, homosexual acts, or erotic art and literature."[25] This is a conclusion of breathtaking scope, the implications of which can be grasped when one realizes that by reducing much of Old Testament sexual ethics to purity concerns and thus lumping many sexual prohibitions with Jewish dietary laws, Countryman is seriously arguing that instead of God showing a hungry Peter a sheet filled with unclean animals and saying "Get up, Peter. Kill and eat" (Acts 10:13), God could have just as easily and validly shown a sexually aroused Peter the same vision of animals and have said, "Get up, Peter. Copulate and be gratified." Since, according to Countryman, there is no more moral prohibition against bestiality than against eating unclean animals, eating pork and having sex with a pig become morally equivalent (as long as the sex is loving and consensual). This is an unlikely interpretation of the biblical record. The core problem, in our understanding, is Countryman's imposition of an alien interpretive lens ("all ethical prohibitions are purity or property violations") through which to view the biblical text, and the unsavory consequences of the analysis result.

Nelson is a good example of how the usage of familiar sounding theological terms is no guarantee of fidelity to traditional theology. His system basically unfolds in the following way: God's work in the world is

---

[25]Countryman, *Dirt, Greed and Sex*, pp. 243-44.

through incarnation. Incarnation (as Nelson uses the word), however, is not centered on the unique life, death and resurrection of Jesus Christ; Christ gets little attention in Nelson's work except as a (vague) moral teacher. Rather, the focus of incarnation is on God doing God's work through incarnation in the lives of human beings. Nelson emphasizes the embodiment of human beings, and a vital part of embodiment is our sexuality. Hence, an important part of God's incarnational work through humanity is through loving human acts that are always embodied, always sexual in broad terms, and which may be and often naturally are sexual in the narrower, genital sense. Nelson talks little of sin but does attribute many or most human ills to a version of the Fall—alienation from our bodies due to the influence of Gnostic dualism, a view promulgated by traditionalistic Christianity.

"Sexual salvation" for Nelson is to be found in breaking down our dualistic alienation from our bodies and living in grace, which is the healing of the breach between the physical and nonphysical aspects of ourselves and the creation of loving communities. Put more crassly, salvation is nothing more than becoming a whole, embodied person who is in touch with the good work God is incarnating through us. In working out the ethical implications of this model, Nelson argues that legalistic prohibitions on sexual intercourse before marriage are passé and should be replaced by personal judgments about loving intention and commitment, that masturbation and the use of erotica and other means of sexual self-discovery are to be celebrated, that those married people who have to make the difficult choice between "genital exclusivity and enduring lifelong commitment"[26] should choose the latter (that is, some people just have to commit adultery to stay married), and for full acceptance of loving and virtuous homosexual practice and that of other sexual variations. All this through a redefinition of incarnation.

The 1991 majority report of the human sexuality study committee of the Presbyterian Church of the USA is easily summarized. Starting with the presumption that the witness of Scripture on matters of sexuality and sexual ethics is internally inconsistent, the authors determined that two ethical/theological concepts should drive all interpretation of the biblical witness regarding sex: *justice* and *love* (two characteristics that have, for

---

[26]Nelson, *Embodiment: An Approach*, p. 149.

many, served as an apt summary of the most salient aspects of God's own character).

Justice and love both have meanings in Christian context that are shaped by the entire web of Christian understandings of God's work in the world, but the authors of this study took a slant on defining each that was (shall we say) innovative in comparison to traditional views—justice was defined as rigid equity between persons, and love was defined in terms of those actions that aid personal self-actualization. This organizing rule then allowed many specific biblical commands to be dismissed as inconsistent with these broader truths and hence not binding; put differently, this rule became the lens allowing the authors to discern the Word of God contained within the Bible, the Word within the word (as opposed to the traditional and evangelical view of the entirety of the Bible constituting the Word of God). The implications of this approach were made very explicit, the most notable of which was that there can be no ban on sexual intercourse for single persons, whether heterosexual or homosexual, because such a rule would be both inequitable (sex for married persons but not for singles is unfair) and damaging to the actualization needs of singles (who have as much a need for embodied, genital love as married persons).

Challenges for Christians

As we bring this book to a close, we are reminded of the importance of a proper understanding of scientific findings and their application to the church's moral debate. We would offer a few closing challenges.

First, we challenge Christians to recognize the role of moral choice in the formation of our very selves. Yet Christians must also remember that because we are fallen, we are inclined to deceive ourselves, to rationalize—after the fact—the wrong behavior to which we have committed ourselves. This is one of the many powerful subtexts of Romans 1: in our rebellion against God and in our captivity, our enslavement to sin, we are quite capable of denying the truth and allowing our "flesh" to dictate the parameters of our understanding. This means that it is essential that we strive to pursue righteous living even when we do not understand it because it can be that in that state when we have been freed by God from the most egregious of our sinful behavior patterns that our moral vision will clear enough for us to be more able to form true ideas. It is a part of our tradition to affirm that we believe so that we might understand; it would be even more accurate to say that we must believe *and obey* so that we might understand.

A second challenge is that Christians are to recognize that efforts to push the church away from its traditional stance on sexual morality are masquerading as faithful Christian scholarship that integrates faith and science. This is particularly true when "science" or "reason" or "human experience" are raised up as requiring modification of the traditional Christian sexual ethic. These discussions take the exact form of discussions about integration of faith and science, and serious error can only be avoided in these areas if a person thoroughly understands and is committed to the truth. We hope that our extended discussion of homosexuality in this book has helped to demonstrate the errors in reasoning of those who would promote change from the traditional Christian sexual ethic.

Third, we challenge Christians to extend the discussion of sexuality and sexual ethics beyond the homosexuality debate to our fundamental vision of the nature of human sexuality.

Coming Full Circle: Summary and Concluding Thoughts on Homosexuality

We have argued that the phenomenon of homosexuality is a pressing area where a proper understanding of the relationship between Christian faith and scientific research is desperately needed. We have argued that the traditional Christian sexual ethic says the following about homosexuality: (1) homosexual behavior violates God's revealed will, (2) homosexual behavior is contrary to God's creational purposes for sexual intimacy, (3) the state of having homosexual desires is of uncertain moral status but certainly must be viewed as a deviation from the Creator's intent for those individuals and must be seen as representing an occasion for sin (just as does heterosexual lust), (4) the origins of homosexual attraction are unclear but grounded ultimately in our human fallenness and rebellion against God, and (5) that there were persons in the New Testament fellowship who were once participants in homosexual practice but who identified with such practices no longer. While foundational, these teachings certainly leave out much that would be beneficial to know about this human condition. If Christians care about the homosexual person, that care should motivate study in this important area. Hence this is a prime area where a Christian engagement (grounded in the Bible's teachings about sexuality and homosexuality) with the fruits of human reason and inquiry holds much promise.

We have argued throughout this book that that possibility has been overshadowed by the reality of "scientific" knowledge about homosexuality being used to batter the church into submission to the views of the world. We recognize that the misuse of science has had a devastating impact on church indecision and warfare over the morality of homosexual behavior, as well as on the spiritual vitality, teaching office and corporate witness of the church.[27] Simply put, the supposed teachings of "science" were and are being used to convince the church that it can no longer hold to the traditional moral judgment regarding homosexual practice. We have directed much of our work to opposing this pressure by reviewing the current state of our knowledge in the areas of prevalence, etiology, status as a mental disorder and possibility of change for the homosexual.

To summarize, the essential claim in discussions about prevalence is that the high prevalence of homosexuality, claimed to be 10% or more of the general population, demands revision of our traditional ethic. The best studies, however, suggest a prevalence rate of between 2 and 3%. More importantly, prevalence has no claim on our ethic, since Christians commonly believe that some sinful life patterns are very common, such as pride, while some are rare, like bestiality.

Claims about the origins of same-sex attraction and homosexuality are at the heart of the homosexuality debate. In various forms the central claim is the following: "If research can persuasively show that the homosexual state is caused by factors beyond the individual's control, especially if the causative factors are biological/genetic in nature, then it would be wrong for the Christian church to condemn homosexual action or lifestyle." Many today assume that that persuasive case has been made and the matter settled.

We would argue that both halves of this "if-then" proposition fail: the case has not been made persuasively, and the "then" clause would not fol-

---

[27]For one explicit discussion of the impact of conflict over sexual ethics on a major denomination, see William J. Abraham, "United Methodists at the End of the Mainline," *First Things*, June-July 1998, pp. 28-33.

low even if the "if" clause were affirmed. The research on the origins of homosexuality is incomplete. We have argued that there is evidence that genetic variables, brain differences and psychological/experiential/familial variables are all involved in the causation of homosexuality. Each of these may, to varying degrees, be *contributing* causes to any specific case of homosexuality. None of these variables has been shown to be causative in the sense understood by the general public — "You have the gene, and thus you have the condition." In any case, such research is fundamentally irrelevant to the Christian ethical case. The only way to exempt homosexuals from the demands of God's Law is to show that they are incapable of responsible choice regarding their actions because of the influence of causative factors — that they are subhuman robots acting without choice because of their condition. Few gay advocates would accept such a depiction of their condition.

Even if the homosexual condition of desiring intimacy and sexual union with a person of the same gender is caused in its entirety by causal factors outside the personal control of the person, that does not constitute moral affirmation of acting on those desires. If it did, the pedophile who desires sex with children, the alcoholic who desires the pursuit of drunkenness, and the person with Antisocial Personality Disorder who desires the thrill of victimization and pain infliction would all have an equal case for moral approval of their exploits. At the broadest level all humans are heirs to a predisposition that we have not chosen and that propels us toward self-destruction and evil — our sinful nature. The plight of the homosexual who has desires and passions that he or she did not choose is in fact the common plight of humanity. We all face the same challenge: how are we to live when what we want is out of accord with what God tells us we should want in this life?

The argument over whether or not homosexuality is a "mental disorder" and, conversely, a "normal lifestyle variant," has also been presumed by some to be of deep relevance to the church's ethical reflection: if mental health professionals declare homosexuality to not be a mental disorder, and in fact to be a healthy lifestyle variant, then how can Christians call it sinful? The discussions on this point are relevant but not central to the point, as many phenomena that are "mental disorders" are not themselves sinful life patterns (such as schizophrenia or panic attacks), and many sinful patterns are not themselves "mental disorders" (such as witchcraft or greed). We have also argued that the evidence that homosexuality is not a psychopathology or developmental abnormality is not as unequivocal as proponents for change have described it.

Arguments about change can also be simply summarized: contemporary science, it is claimed, has shown that there are no effective therapies to produce change by which the homosexual can become heterosexual, and hence the church's moral condemnation of those who act in a manner they cannot willingly change is wrong. Again, this "if-then" clause is wrong on both sides. The research actually shows a change effect of modest size, approximating that for such vexing conditions as the three examples above—pedophilia, alcoholism and Antisocial Personality Disorder. Initial change may occur for only a minority, and relapses among those who change at all may be frequent, but that is not the same as saying that none can change. It appears to us that profound change of orientation occurs infrequently. But again, this is irrelevant to the call of the gospel because conversion to heterosexuality, while a testimony to God's grace, is nevertheless not required for faithful discipleship. The change minimally demanded by the gospel is not conversion to heterosexuality but chastity in one's state of life. And that call, costly though it may be, stands as a possibility for any of us.

We have dealt here only with the "scientific" arguments advanced against the church's traditional ethic. There are of course biblical, theological, sociological, strategic and political arguments in play in this great debate, but those are beyond the scope of this book. The issue of homosexuality is, we believe, by and in itself a rather isolated and peripheral issue, but it is a battlefield on which other much more weighty theological and biblical concerns are being debated; it is an issue that has the potential, already partially realized, to splinter and divide the body of Christ. Christians must attend carefully to it.

Why should faithful Christians continue to stress the traditional moral norms, insisting on full sexual intimacy as a gift to be shared in heterosexual marriage alone? Why should faithful Christians continue to stress the traditional Christian judgment that homosexual sexual intimacy is always wrong? Because Christians are asked to say no to certain types of sexual activity in order to say yes to a certain ordering of our lives that is ordained by God to be morally good. Such a life involves many elements alien to the modern mind—self-denial, sacrifice, but above all a willingness to admit our guilt and unworthiness before God, a willingness to plead for mercy and forgiveness, and a willingness to follow Christ in obedience to his revealed will. Our goal must be an unending pursuit of holiness of life. Our goal must be the transformation of the human character from its fallen condition, in which nothing good dwells, into the likeness of Jesus Christ himself. Sexual purity is an integral part of loving and giving glory to God and of the transformation of our character.

Discussion Questions

1. Why is it important to understand human sexuality and sexual behavior within the context of all of Scripture (Creation, Fall, Redemption, Glorification) rather than merely in the light of specific texts studied in isolation?

2. Do you agree that a Christian sexual ethic is an ethic of obedience, loyalty, principle, caution and virtue? Why or why not? Are there other dimensions you would add?

3. How compelling and conclusive are the findings from science? Do these findings lead us to conclude that the church can no longer hold to the traditional moral judgment regarding homosexual behavior?

4. In what ways are the concepts of self-denial and the pursuit of holiness relevant to the topic of homosexuality?

5. Is the debate about homosexuality simply a debate about homosexuality, or is it about broader issues of greater importance to the church? Put another way, do two people who seem to agree theologically in every way *except* their views of the morality of homosexual behavior *really* agree on all those other matters?

Index

Stanton L. Jones is provost and professor of psychology at Wheaton College, Wheaton, Illinois. During his tenure as chair of the psychology department (1984-1996), he led the development of Wheaton's Doctor of Psychology program in clinical psychology. He received his B.S. in psychology from Texas A & M University in 1976, and his M.A. (1978) and Ph.D. (1981) degrees in clinical psychology from Arizona State University. He is a member of the American Psychological Association and serves on the Council of Representatives, the central governing body of the APA, representing Division 36, the Psychology of Religion division.

Dr. Jones authored the lead article on "Religion and Psychology" for the *Encyclopedia of Psychology*, jointly published in 2000 by the American Psychological Association and Oxford University Press. His article in the March 1994 *American Psychologist*, titled "A Constructive Relationship for Religion with the Science and Profession of Psychology: Perhaps the Boldest Model Yet," was a call for greater respect for and cooperation with religion by secular psychologists. Dr. Jones has written, with his wife, Brenna, a five-book series on sex education in the Christian family called *God's Design for Sex*. He is coauthor with Richard Butman of *Modern Psychotherapies*.

Mark A. Yarhouse is a licensed clinical psychologist in the Commonwealth of Virginia and assistant professor of psychology at Regent University in Virginia Beach. He received B.A. degrees in philosophy and art from Calvin College in 1990 and M.A. degrees in clinical psychology (1993) and theological studies (1997) from Wheaton College. He completed the Psy.D. in clinical psychology at Wheaton in 1998.

Dr. Yarhouse chaired an American Psychological Association symposium titled *Gays, Ex-Gays, Ex-Ex-Gays: Examining Key Religious, Ethical and Diversity Issues* which brought together professionals from the gay community and the conservative religious community to discuss professional services for persons who experience same-sex attraction. He has published articles in such journals as *Professional Psychology: Research and Practice, Psychotherapy*, and *Journal of Psychology and Christianity*. He serves on the editorial boards of *Journal of Family Violence, The Family Journal, Journal of Psychology and Theology*, and *Marriage and Family: A Christian Journal*.

He is currently participating in a three-year think tank—the Reaffirming Marriage Initiative—sponsored by the Ethics and Public Policy Center in Washington, D.C.